English Public Schools

1 Canterbury
2 Sherborne
3 Winchester
4 Shrewsbury
5 Uppingham
6 Rugby
7 Oundle
8 Harrow
9 Christ's Hospital
10 Charterhouse
11 St Paul's
12 Westminster
13 Dulwich
14 Cheltenham
15 Marlborough
16 Radley
17 Lancing
18 Bradfield
19 Wellington
20 Haileybury
21 Clifton
22 Blundell's
23 Ampleforth
24 Sedbergh
25 Eton

James McConnell

English Public Schools

W·W·Norton & Company
New York   London

to Meg

First published in Great Britain 1985
by The Herbert Press Limited,
46 Northchurch Road, London N1 4EJ
Designed by Pauline Harrison

First American edition, 1985

Published simultaneously in Canada
by Penguin Books Canada Limited,
2801 John Street, Markham, Ontario L3R 1B4

Library of Congress Cataloging in
Publication Data

McConnell, James.
   English public schools.
   1. Public schools, Endowed (Great Britain)—
Directories.   2. Public schools, Endowed (Great
Britain)—History.   I. Title.
L915.M33   1985   373.2'22'02541   85 = 10575

ISBN 0-393-02244-7

W.W. Norton & Company, Inc.,
500 Fifth Avenue, New York, NY 10110.
W.W. Norton & Company, Ltd., ·
37 Great Russell Street, London WC1B 3NU

Printed in Great Britain

PREVIOUS PAGE   Sherborne School
The School Courts and Headmaster's Wing
(courtesy John Catt Ltd)

1 2 3 4 5 6 7 8 9 0

Contents

Author's note

The author wishes to thank the Headmasters, assistant masters and pupils who made him welcome and talked so interestingly about their schools. The twenty-five descriptions are all based on visits made during 1984 and, though brief, may give some idea of the schools as they were in that particular year. In a short account it was not possible to cover everything but it is hoped that the most important features and the individual character of each school will become apparent. None of the descriptions or opinions given in this book were dictated by the Headmasters or personnel of the schools but are the author's own independent views.

A page of more specific information is provided at the end of each chapter, with the titles of books that deal with the subject in more detail. This information was checked and up-dated at the beginning of 1985 just before the book went to press. For readers not familiar with Public Schools a definition of some of the terms used is given on page 218.

Preamble

THIS BOOK TAKES THE READER ON A TOUR OF TWENTY-FIVE renowned English Public Schools, describing their setting and environment, the style of their buildings, the facilities they offer for study and recreation, and the way they are changing in the last decades of the twentieth century. Though they have much in common, each has its own special character and one of the aims of the author has been to bring out this individual quality.

Britain is fortunate in possessing two great systems of education, and one of the blessings of democratic freedom is that they can exist side by side. On one hand is the immense structure of the so-called State system, which has been in existence now for almost a hundred and fifty years and ensures that every child in the land can receive free schooling. In State schools nearly ten million children are taught by over half a million teachers at a cost of over £14,000 million a year. Britain being a free country, parents are also allowed to send their sons and daughters to schools other than those established by the public authorities, so there are more than 2,500 independent schools with over 550,000 pupils. Such schools provide 70 per cent of the boarding places available in this country. Within the independent sector there is a group of 230 schools which are members of the Headmasters' Conference. They are sometimes described as the Public Schools. (A list of HMC schools will be found on page 220.)

Though the Public School is a primarily English institution there are Public Schools in Scotland, Ireland and Wales as well. Together they form a unique network unparalleled anywhere in the world and they are the envy of many other countries. The earliest can trace their origins back fourteen hundred years. Nearly all were generously endowed by philanthropic founders and have attracted considerable benefactions in recent times. Some are set in superb environments and many have buildings of outstanding architectural merit. Though they are linked in a number of associations, each one is an independent entity under its own governing body.

'Public School' is a misleading term which lingers on though it has become out of date and the schools themselves would prefer to be known by some other name. The term first came into use when certain local schools began to attract pupils from all over the country and became in a sense national institutions. They were 'public' because anyone could send a child there, not just local people. Victorian parents sent sons rather than daughters and so for a long time a Public School was synonymous with a boys' boarding school. The reputation of these schools conferred a certain cachet for life on their pupils. What set them apart was that they had shared an experience only available to a minority; they had left home and family to live in an enclosed society under spartan conditions, where regimes and rituals of almost tribal severity prevailed. There were many unhappy boys but those who came through had one great asset; they had learned early in life to be a member of a community. So grew up the notion of 'the Public School boy' with all the mystique which that implied.

Rugby School master in Dr Arnold's time
by C.W. Andrews 1842 (*Geoffrey Creighton Studio*)

The House system is a feature common to Public Schools and the House means much more than a building in which from fifty to ninety boys or girls have their habitat. It was Arnold of Rugby who first gave the Housemaster a pastoral role, so that he came to be the most important influence in a boy's school life. Loyalty to House often surpasses loyalty to school, and parents regard the choice of a House as no less important than the choice of a school. The system has the great advantage of breaking a large community into smaller, more personal units, and for this reason is adopted by many day schools.

The greatest change in the traditional Public Schools is not common to all. It was John Dancy at Marlborough who first admitted girls, but only into the Sixth Form. It was regarded as a revolutionary innovation, though Bedales had been happily educating boys and girls together since its foundation by

J.H. Badley in 1893. Ninety-two years later about half the schools in this book, once purely for boys, are admitting girls. And much of Badley's philosophy is now accepted – mutual understanding between the sexes, a more informal relationship between teacher and pupil, discipline based on co-operation and commonsense rather than authority, the ability to work on your own, a strong emphasis on music, art, drama and manual work. The schools accommodate the girls in different ways, either giving them their own House, or dispersing them among boys' Houses, or lodging them with families nearby. Wherever they are they have greatly changed the atmosphere of the place. But even where there are no girls the Public Schools have

Bedales School (*photo James McConnell*)

changed. The out-worn traditions have been abandoned, though some retain their picturesque and eccentric uniforms. The more friendly relationship between teachers and pupils extends to the senior and junior boys. Beating of boys by boys is a thing of the past and fagging in its old form has disappeared in the face of public hostility. Prefects or Monitors have become more like counsellors and less like policemen.

One tradition which has not changed is the maintenance of high academic standards, which is inevitably linked to the General Certificate of Education. Everywhere the curriculum is dominated by GCE, an external examination for which pupils are entered at Ordinary Level (O Level) when they are about 15 and at Advanced Level (A Level) when they are about 17, with the best candidates also taking Scholarship (S) papers. Most of the schools have a curriculum like a pyramid with a broad range of subjects for the first two years, a narrower range during the year before O Level, and specialization on three or four A Level subjects for the last two years. The acquisition of high Grades is now so essential as a qualification for Higher Education and also for employment that parents demand good results. As they are the clients and pay the fees the schools try to deliver the goods. But without exception they do their best to broaden the Sixth Form curriculum with stimulating and remarkably varied non-examinable subjects, often under the heading of General Studies. Though they do not show up in any table of results these courses can be the most truly educational in the broad sense. Statistics of examination results have to be cautiously interpreted and comparisons can be odious, but the Public Schools can justifiably claim to be preserving a high standard of scholarship and to be contributing a good proportion of the trained brains so urgently needed in a modern society.

Essential on every staff now are the Careers and University Entrance masters and no school is complete without a room set aside for this, equipped with reference books, guides, pamphlets, statistics and maybe a computer. Without the aid of ISCO (Independent Schools Careers Organisation) the task would be impossible but even so it is of mammoth proportions and calls for real dedication. University entrance is more complex than ever, with everything thrown into confusion by Oxford's unilateral decision to make candidates take their exam in the fourth term of A Level work. University entrance advisers have difficulty in persuading parents that Oxbridge is not the be-all and end-all. The pattern is changing and whereas more Public School pupils than ever before are going on to degree courses fewer are going to Oxford and Cambridge and more to other Universities or Polytechnics – where they may well find courses more suited to their needs. Careers masters are also trying to persuade parents and pupils that industry has as much to offer as the so-called professions and that, as the Harrow booklet 'Sixth Form Choices' puts it, 'career patterns of the past do not necessarily reflect the needs and aspirations of the future'.

The schools in this survey are not intended to be a sort of Top Twenty-five. They were chosen to provide a good geographical spread and the interest of variety. Neither the HMC nor any other official body had anything to do with the selection. The title precluded the Scottish, Irish and Welsh schools, and it will be immediately apparent that some of the best English schools have been spared the author's attentions. In the same way it was decided to limit this survey to predominantly boys' schools and leave the many excellent girls' schools in the HMC to some other publication. All the schools included have some renown and each illustrates a different facet of the whole picture. Though they are not taken strictly in the order of their foundation, it will be possible to identify some of the principal milestones in the development of the Public School from AD 600 to 1985. Each school has been visited personally and the author has had the enlightening experience of conversing with a couple of dozen leading Headmasters. Talking to pupils was always interesting, but one has to take their comments with a pinch of salt, allowing for the irreverence and light-hearted cynicism of the young on the subject of any 'establishment'. Similarly, the opinions of parents have to be heard with caution, for they are usually subjective. Mothers and fathers tend to see schools through the eyes of their children; if the child does well it's a good school, if the child fails the school has failed.

The tour starts with the King's School, Canterbury, which traces its roots back to the year 600, when St Augustine founded his monastery there. Sherborne has roots almost as ancient but it was at Winchester that the first school was founded on a pattern that was to be followed by many others in later centuries. Shrewsbury was guided from the seventeenth to the nineteenth century by a triumvirate of great Headmasters, Butler, Kennedy and Moss; but it was Arnold of Rugby who established the Public School as a respectable institution. Thring of Uppingham probably did more to humanize boarding schools than any other man; Sanderson at Oundle saw the need to adapt education to an industrial society and Vaughan of Harrow saw the value of organized games as a means of channelling excess energy. Next come Christ's Hospital and Charterhouse, which moved out of London in search of a more salubrious environment in the country, by contrast with Westminster, St Paul's and Dulwich which stayed in the metropolis. The next five schools were founded within a dozen years of each other: Cheltenham, Marlborough, Radley, Bradfield and Lancing all started in the 1840s, the last being the

Christ's Hospital. Reflection of the Quad in brass tuba during band practice
(*photo Neil Fleming*)

English lesson at Westminster School (*photo Bahman Sanai*)

flagship of the Woodard Schools. The opening of Wellington in 1853 was a national event, while Haileybury and Clifton were both founded in the year 1862. Blundell's, 175 miles west of London, has for 380 years served the needs of the West Country and bears the name of the Tiverton mercer who endowed it. Ampleforth is situated away north of York but draws Roman Catholics from all over Britain, whilst its near neighbour, Sedbergh, was founded by a Provost of Eton in 1525 to provide a grammar school education for scholars in the North of England. The largest and most famous of them all, Eton College, has been placed last so that the reader can compare it with the other schools and judge whether or not it deserves its world-wide renown.

Eton has been attended by Kings and Princes, not to mention Dukes, Lords and Knights by the dozen, but the sons of the top family in the land were not sent there. The privilege of educating Princes Charles, Andrew and Edward was given to Gordonstoun, where Prince Philip himself had been to school. Being in Scotland, Gordonstoun does not come within the scope of this book, though it is a most unusual and interesting school. In the Nazi Germany of the early 1930s Kurt Hahn regarded as a matter of urgency the need to educate young people in independence of judgement and in strength of purpose; and to train them in protection of the weak, recognition of the rights of the less fortunate, and the worth of a single human life. He saw the tradition of the great English Public Schools as a framework within which he could launch a new kind of education for the twentieth century. To achieve his ideal he came to Britain and founded Gordonstoun near Inverness on the Moray Firth.

Gordonstoun. The school yacht, 'Sea Spirit' (*Gordonstoun School*)

The King's School, Canterbury

520 BOARDING BOYS

94 DAY BOYS

53 BOARDING GIRLS

16 DAY GIRLS (Sixth Form)

THIS SCHOOL CAN TRACE ITS ORIGINS BACK TO THE YEAR AD 600, FOR its roots and daily life are embedded in the history of Christian England. In 597 St Augustine was sent from Rome by Pope Gregory the Great. He landed at Pegwell Bay and came on to Canterbury, and his first night was spent at Stablegate, still to be found behind the school shop.

Canterbury had first become important because it was here that Watling Street, the great Roman military road from Dover to London, crossed the head of the Stour estuary. Christianity had come to England with the Romans and even before St Augustine arrived there was a church at Canterbury. The Pope's emissary, who was made welcome by the Anglo-Saxon King Ethelbert, founded two separate establishments, the Monastery of St Augustine and the Cathedral of Christchurch. The Cathedral was burnt down in the great fire of 1067 and rebuilt by the first two Norman Archbishops, Lanfranc and Anselm. The martyrdom of Archbishop Thomas Becket, hacked to death in 1170 because he had defied a tyrant, made Canterbury Cathedral famous throughout the Christian world. The shrine of St Thomas became the goal of pilgrims and has been celebrated in literature from Chaucer's *Canterbury Tales* to T.S. Eliot's *Murder in the Cathedral*.

It is generally assumed that when St Augustine founded the Cathedral and Monastery he also founded the grammar school which still flourishes. Proof that a school was there in pre-Norman times is provided by the monk Eadmer, who recorded that all the boys were by custom flogged with knotted scourges of bull's hide five days before Christmas. However, King's School does not owe its name to Ethelbert but to Henry VIII. When he abolished St Augustine's along with the other monasteries he established a New Foundation in 1541. The Headmaster of the old 'School of the Archbishop and the City' became head of the new school, which was to be regulated by the Dean and Chapter. Under its Statutes it was to provide for fifty King's Scholars, 'poor boys both destitute of the aid of friends and endowed with minds born and apt for learning'. Archbishop Cranmer decreed: 'If the Gentleman's son be apt for learning, let him be admitted.' At a price, presumably.

For three hundred years the King's School served the needs of the men of

A class outside The Grange (*photo Campbell McCallum*)

Kent, sending forth scholars to Cambridge and Oxford who became ornaments of the professions both temporal and spiritual. Its first great expansion came when the moderation of the eighteenth century gave way to the vigour of the nineteenth, and Great Britain became the power-house of the world. But it was under F.J. Shirley, Headmaster from 1935 to 1967, that King's became recognized as a great school. Prior to his appointment he wrote to the Dean, Dr Hewlett Johnson, famous as the Red Dean, 'My dear Mr. Dean, I hope you will have the patience to read what is going to be a very long letter.' It ran to 3,500 words and pointed out some shortcomings of the establishment, but he still got the job. When he arrived the school was in deficit, there were no assets and it was running at a loss; when he left its finances were sound and numbers had gone up from 200 to 500. He had initiated extensive rebuilding, including a School Hall, deemed essential by any self-respecting headmaster. During World War II he took the school to Carlyon Bay Hotel in Cornwall, where the vast garage was called 'Cath' and the scholars still wore their gowns. They thus escaped the 'Baedeker raids' of June 1942 when fourteen bombs were dropped in the Cathedral Precincts.

A recent new boy wrote home to his parents after the first couple of weeks: 'I am settling down well here. There is a Cathedral in the School grounds.' In fact, the school buildings have always lain within the precincts, and the King's School lives and works under the towering mass of the great Cathedral. The old city walls belt it in on one side, the City of Canterbury on the other. Here there is no escape for the eye as at Charterhouse or Sedbergh, the straying glance encounters only flint, stone, Tudor brick. School buildings, many of them adaptations of ancient structures, are enmeshed with the houses and offices of the Dean and Chapter. Here and there anonymous ruins are a reminder of how ephemeral are all man's institutions, and at the Canonical Hours the great bell chivvies the scurrying boys and girls. Chattering and perhaps unaware they crowd past the reminders of our history. In that room above St Augustine's Gate, Queen Henrietta Maria, en route from Dover to London, spent the first night of her married life. The Dark Entry passes through Prior Selling's fifteenth-century gateway, where, the *Ingoldsby Legends* tell us, a nun was walled up. The Norman staircase leading up to the Library dates from 1150, Meister Omer's house bears the name of a Dutchman who was in the service of the Priory from 1240 to 1280 and Walpole House stands on the site of the old Archbishop's Palace. The housemaster's study is in the porch, now bricked up, where the four Knights armed before going to murder Thomas Becket on the altar steps. A covered way, the Pentize, was the self-same route by which Canterbury Pilgrims approached the rooms named Heaven and Hell.

In 1976 a whole new chunk of history came within the school's orbit, when St Augustine's Abbey, outside the City walls, was acquired against fierce competition. There on 20 May 1978 School and Chapter celebrated the 1000th anniversary of the dedication of the High Altar.

In 1972 a development of equal historical importance occurred; the first girls were admitted into the Sixth Form of this school which for centuries had been reserved for boys. Now there are about seventy-five of them, fifty of whom are boarders. They are assigned to one or other of the boys' Houses where they have a share of a study and participate in all activities except manly sports. They sleep in one of the two girls' boarding houses, where they share bed-sitting rooms.

The theme throughout the school is the adaptation of old buildings to modern educational uses. A former medieval barn is now a central dining-room run on a self-service basis, the new Cleary Art Centre is in the old refectory of the 1270 Dominican Priory with wood and metal workshops in the former vaults, while access to the Computer Room is through Archbishop Parker's 1561 Gate.

The boarding Houses vary enormously. Seven of them are in the Precinct, together with two Houses for day boys, while Tradescant and Broughton are in St Augustine's Abbey. They have all been adapted to make the maximum use of space, Luxmore being the newest and most modern, Galpin's the most quirky. Meister Omer's is still organized with dormitories and work hall. The others have work/play rooms on the ground floor, most have libraries and all have TV and video. In one House a former dining hall has been converted into three storeys of studies, tapering into the apex of the ceiling where they look out through the old clerestory windows. Some of the studies in Tradescant, in the old Augustine Monastery, are evocative. For instance, that of Paolo Mondadori has one wall consisting entirely of a Gothic window.

Sherborne School. Painted effigy of Edward VI (*courtesy John Catt Ltd*)

The King's School, Canterbury (*photo Campbell McCallum*)

Winchester College entrance. Aquatint by Havell after Westall, from Ackermann's *Public Schools* 1816 (*British Museum*)

Broadly speaking, boys in their first year work in study rooms which have individual desk spaces and sleep in dormitories with up to sixteen beds, some of them bunk beds. They graduate to bed-sitters occupied by four, three, two and finally one.

Does this unique setting with its constant reminder of the past make an impression on the boys and girls who live and work here? The effect is probably subliminal, for boys especially come to take these things for granted. But a former pupil discovered in the death cell of Sachsenhausen concentration camp that the memory of such an environment saved his sanity.

The Cathedral is known familiarly as 'Cath', yet its nearness to something that is greater than itself makes the school less conscious of its corporate identity. The setting encourages individuality and aesthetic values and perhaps also humility. Maybe that is why King's School is not noted for producing politicians – OKSs are reluctant to toe any party line – though it is said that 'one finds King's men wherever individuality matters'. Today's pupils honour their writers – Christopher Marlowe, Walter Pater, Hugh Walpole, Somerset Maugham. To judge by his book *Of Human Bondage* you would think Maugham had hated his school days, yet he became a benefactor, endowing a Scholarship for the sons of manual workers. He left his collection of books to the school and asked to be buried near the Cathedral. His ashes lie in Galpin garden just outside the Library.

The playing fields outside the city were acquired by two shrewd Headmasters. Blore's Field and Birley's Field are respectively five and ten minutes walk from the Precinct. The Boat Club has recently acquired water at Sturry gravel pits which provides a sheltered course of 1500 metres. The Eight, competing in boats with names like The Wife of Bath, is now one of the best in the country. King's School also prides itself on its Rugby and Hockey teams, while in 1983 the Cricket XI had seven wins and only one loss. The success as Captain of England of David Gower, in the team 1971–74, has been a fillip. There are also cross-country running and a dozen other minor sports. Pupils are expected to take exercise several times a week, especially in the Middle and Lower School.

The academic tradition is strong, and in the past twenty-five years pupils have won two hundred Awards at Cambridge and Oxford. An important feature is the system of Tutors. Each House has masters allocated to it, the number varying from one to six according to the whim of the Housemaster, though there is always one resident. In addition every pupil is assigned to an academic Tutor who takes a personal interest and sees him or her every week for a Tutor Session. In the Sixth Form the school divides almost equally between the Humanities and Science. Scientists have seventeen laboratories at their disposal, including five new ones. History is, not surprisingly, a strong subject, and in recent years Economics and Politics have yielded very good results. Last year half the candidates for Cambridge and Oxford were successful, and in Advanced Level GCE the pass rate was 92 per cent, with over half the candidates achieving a Grade A or B.

Croquet at St Augustine's. Fyndon's Gate (1309) in the background
(*The King's School, Canterbury*)

Practising on the Green Court for a
sponsored go-kart race in aid of charity
(© *The Guardian 1983*)

RIGHT Crossing the River Stour by the
mediaeval Blackfriars' refectory, now the
Arts Centre (*photo Anthony Wattenbach*)

Music is the strongest non-academic activity, and King's runs a symphony orchestra of seventy players, a School Band and four choirs, one of a hundred voices. As befits the school of Marlowe, drama is also well supported, and the two activities combine for the traditional festival of King's Week in July.

King's School retains other traditions. The uniform of the boys dates from Edwardian times – wing collar, black jacket and grey trousers (striped on Sundays) – and King's Scholars still wear their gowns for lessons. The monitors are inducted by the Dean in the Cathedral, wear purple gowns on formal occasions, and are allowed to carry black swagger sticks. For Speeches the most senior pupils wear Court dress.

The Dean and Chapter are a constant presence and perhaps tend to influence the Headmaster too much in decisions which he should take without interference. But in this very ecclesiastical environment religion is not over-emphasized. The object is to arouse awareness rather than indoctrinate. However, there is a compulsory service for the whole school every other Sunday in the quire of the Cathedral. On other Sundays the Lower School attends its own service, while the Upper School chooses between sung Communion and a talk. There is voluntary Communion daily in one of the school's three chapels and a compulsory Assembly in the Shirley Hall. It is a privilege of King's pupils to be confirmed by the Archbishop.

The admission of girls into the Sixth Form in the 1970s has done much to create the present ethos. They have no uniform, being merely required to

Cardinal Hume after preaching
the Commemoration Sermon
in the Cathedral
(© *The Guardian 1983*)

wear skirts rather than trousers and clothing that is grey, of whatever shape and shade. Perhaps it is this greater freedom that makes them seem more poised and mature than the boys. They are tolerantly amused by the boys' structured attitudes and the importance they attach to team games. The fact that some of them are monitors has accelerated the erosion of the old barriers between age-groups. The authoritarian attitude of monitors has given way to a more 'pastoral' role towards younger boys. But in some Houses the boy who is not keen on games can still feel very out of things.

Despite its distinguished history this is not a rich school. It is now nearly sixty years since Lady Milner gave her sixteenth-century house and the tithe barn of St Augustine's Monastery, which were opened as a prep school by Rudyard Kipling in 1927. In recent years £1 million has been raised by a sale of land and it is hoped to raise another £500,000 by Appeal. It is largely its Charitable Status that enables the King's School to give away £300,000 per annum in scholarships and other financial aid.

The King's School, Canterbury

ADDRESS Canterbury, Kent CT1 2ES

FOUNDATION AD 600, refounded 1541 by King Henry VIII

GOVERNING BODY The Dean and Chapter of Canterbury Cathedral + 13 other Governors

TITLE OF HEAD AND NUMBER OF TEACHING STAFF Headmaster + 74 (excluding visiting teachers)

TOTAL NUMBER OF PUPILS 700

NUMBER IN SIXTH FORM 355

NUMBER OF ADVANCED LEVEL CHOICES AVAILABLE 25

NAMES OF FORMS (i) Shell (ii) Remove (iii) 5a and 5b (iv) 6b (v) 6a

PRINCIPAL GAMES, BY TERMS *Autumn* Rugby *Lent* Hockey *Summer* Cricket, Rowing

NAMES OF HOUSES
Boarding Walpole, The Grange, School House, Galpin's, Luxmore, Meister Omer's, Tradescant, Broughton
Day Marlowe, Mitchison
Holding Lattergate

APPLICATION AND ENTRY Registration at any time. Entry for boys at 13 +, girls 16 +

SCHOLARSHIPS, ETC.
15 King's Scholarships from 33% to 100% of fees
Lord Milner Memorial Scholarships
Greaves Scholarships
Several Exhibitions
8 Music Scholarships and discretionary Awards

TOTAL ANNUAL ALLOCATION FOR SCHOLARSHIPS, ETC. £300,000

BOOK *A History of the King's School Canterbury* by D.L. Edwards

Sherborne School

SHERBORNE IS SITUATED IN A SALIENT OF DORSET WHICH JUTS NORTH-ward into Somerset. Town and school are surrounded by low hills and an intimate landscape where villages snuggle, bearing names like Ryme Intrinsica, Mintern Magna, Compton Pauncefoot. This county lies at the heart of ancient Britain. Indeed, King Arthur had his 'court' here in the eighth century, and legend has it that he received his very rudimentary education at the school run by Benedictine monks beside the sheer bourn, a glassy, cool, translucent stream which gave the town its name. It is a fact that his two brothers are buried here. London is 120 miles distant. Two important centres, Bournemouth and Bristol, are within fifty miles. The nearest town with any aspiration to be industrial is Yeovil, five miles away, but it is hardly noted for dark satanic mills.

The school itself touches and intermingles with the town. Cheap Street, an amicable thoroughfare with the picturesque bustle of an operatic set, is a

The Staff Common Room, from Cheap Street (*photo Angus Scott Brown*)

mere hundred yards from 'the Courts' (the old Fives Courts have vanished). Several of the boarding Houses are embedded in the town, one of them recently converted from a hotel. Sherborne Abbey, once a Benedictine chapel, forms a background to the south, its tower looming over the original school building and the former cloisters, its peaceable bell scattering quarters day and night on town and gown – a powerful and constant presence. The services which the school attends in the Abbey, such as Commemoration at the end of the Summer Term, are truly grand and memorable occasions.

The hub of the school is the Courts, a gravelled quadrangle bounded by buildings in the soft tones of Ham stone – School House, Chapel, Library and Carrington schoolrooms. Beyond it are the most venerable buildings, the 1560 original School House, the 1606 Dining Hall of the Royal School and the 1670 Oak Room, each offering its own subtle tone to the colour pattern. A reminder of even earlier occupants is the Norman Undercroft. Dating from the thirteenth century it has been converted into a reading room of marvellous style and atmosphere. The old Methodist Hall, sandwiched between town and gown, has recently been purchased. It will be used for concerts, lectures, plays, films, etc., and will be equipped with modern facilities. When ready it will provide another asset shared between the townspeople and the boys. Sherborne has modernized in other ways. Among a score of projects carried out in the last ten years one is of special note. The former gymnasium was converted into a central dining hall run on a cafeteria system, and a new Sports Hall was built nearby containing a deck-level swimming pool, squash courts and two large games areas. All this is shared with other schools and the local community.

Like all schools Sherborne suffered its vicissitudes. In 1889 numbers dropped from 280 to 140 when the Headmaster was sued by a master for libel, the staff turned against him and a senior Housemaster was sacked. The growth of the school in the twentieth century can be gauged from the figure of 221 Old Shirburnians killed in World War I and 242 in World War II.

Sherborne today is a school of 650 pupils, all boys and only twenty of them day boys. As you enter the Courts and see them going about their daily routine in their orderly and purposeful way, you have the feeling that God's in his heaven, all's right with the world. In fact, the dust and turmoil of the rebellious 1960s have settled and most boys appear ready to support the Headmaster when he proposes that the school's object shall be the Pursuit of Excellence. Of course Sherborne, like all schools, has its petty criminals and they may still get beaten for their misdeeds – though not by another boy. And not all Shirburnians have been happy at school. In *The Loom of Youth*, which Alec Waugh wrote in six weeks at the age of 17, he painted an unhappy picture of his own school days, but he nevertheless presented the manuscript to Sherborne in 1965.

It is not for male chauvinistic reasons that Sherborne does not admit girls. Sherborne Girls' School is close but not too close for comfort. Many activities are shared. On a formal basis girls participate in Sixth Form general studies and share some teaching with the boys. Drama and music provide meeting grounds. Less formally, boys and girls may often be seen strolling arm in arm or meeting in Cheap Street to make dates. These attachments are by mutual consent kept at a temperate level and passionate affairs are rare. Restrictions on girls entering boys' Houses and rooms are kept to a minimum and the girls share the boys' Junior Common Room with its bar and electronic 'Scrambler'.

Accommodation is in nine boarding Houses, each of about seventy boys. The Houses are individual and distinct units, communities in themselves with their own traditions. Each is presided over by a resident Housemaster. Nowadays he has several Tutors allocated to help him, one of whom lives in. They supervise the work and other activities of their share of boys. So now every master has some involvement in a boys' House and therefore a better knowledge of and more contact with boys. The Head of House works closely with the Housemaster and has perhaps four House Prefects to help him. Hallkeepers take on lesser responsibilities.

The change from separate catering in Houses to central feeding has altered the house-orientated life of the school. Now all boys go to the Dining Hall for the three main meals. There are two sittings and boys sit not by Houses but as they choose. Masters come in to join them for the midday meal. Apart from meals the bulk of a boy's time is spent in his House and there he does most of his prepared work and private study. Accommodation varies. In most Houses the junior boys have day rooms with small partitioned cubby-hole desks which give them some privacy, and they sleep in dormitories. Then they graduate to studies which hold four, three, two or one occupant. Some Houses have study-bedrooms, others have living studies only and dormitories for all. Some, for instance School House, are ancient and historic, whereas The Digby is a converted luxury hotel.

The playing fields lie to the south-west, about fifty acres set against an agreeable background of low hills with green or wooded slopes. This surrounding landscape lends itself to cross-country running, though the main emphasis is on Rugby, Hockey and Cricket. Games are organized on two levels. The best performers are trained as an élite on a school basis under the best coaches. The rest play for their Houses, joined by the 'bloods' for inter-House competitions. The system is successful and Sherborne expect to win most of their school matches. In 1984 the Cricket XI lost only one match. Today games are not regarded as so important as in days gone by and the more gentle skills are gaining ground.

Music features very prominently. Twenty-one music Scholarships and Exhibitions are available at any one time. There are twenty-four teachers and the Music School has emphasized its pre-eminence by taking over the house intended as the Headmaster's residence. Sherborne acts as the centre for the Dorset Opera Society, and every year the school hosts and participates in an opera (*Don Carlos* in 1984) which involves boys and girls, former pupils and top performers, even from the Continent. This stimulates all musical

The Headmaster inspecting cadets, from *The Shirburnian* 1983 (*photo John Rees*)

activities in the school; there are two orchestras, two bands and three choirs.

The Art School is a rather disappointing building. However, it does not seem to quench inspiration as the seventeen O Level and the three A Level candidates in 1984 *all* passed the examination.

The teaching staff, excluding Music, numbers seventy-two. Only three of them are aged over 50, so on the whole they are forward-looking and innovative, and the Headmaster, in making new appointments, has given priority to raising the academic standard. A Director of Studies oversees all the teaching and the aim is to keep the curriculum broad for as long as possible and to stress the value of subjects which are not for the GCE examination. In the Lower School boys of different ability are mixed for most subjects and only streamed for Maths and French. Wednesday morning is a Creative Morning for all, offering Drama, Music and Art. In the Sixth Form all are required to take a course in English Literature as well as devoting three periods a week to General Studies. To counter the present-day decline in reading, boys are required to work through reading lists. The English department allocate books to House libraries and this reading is supervised by Tutors. The School Library has 15,000 volumes, and Sherborne is currently spending £8,000 a year on books, which is higher than many larger schools. Those studying a modern language spend one term in the appropriate country, living with a family and probably attending the same school as the children. This very broadening experience is threatened by the new Oxford entry exam in the fourth Sixth Form term. Sherborne linguists also take the Institute of Lin-

guists' exam in the Lower Sixth. An interesting development is the introduction of Theology as a main subject. It has produced good results for
University entrance, and more Shirburnians are now going for Ordination.
But on a more temporal level, the computer boom has not been allowed to get
out of hand; the seven consols lurk under the chapel in the former Vestry,
presided over by a pre-Raphaelite painting of Love and Purity.

The visible evidence of academic success is good and on a rising graph
line. In the last two years Sherborne won twelve and eight Oxbridge Awards
respectively which, related to numbers in the Sixth Form, puts it high in the
list of schools in the UK. In the same two years, the overall pass rate was 90
per cent or better, and the percentage of boys gaining A, B and C grades was
over 60 per cent. Sherborne thus shows that, though it is reputed to aim at
lifting the solid middle-of-the-road boy, it can also launch the high flyer.
The emphasis has changed greatly in this respect. In the past it was perhaps a
somewhat physical and oppressively games-conscious school where the less
sporting intellectual boy suffered cruelly. Now the atmosphere is tolerant
and studious, and the purpose of being at school is seen as qualifying yourself
for a job.

The school uniform is uneccentric – grey flannels, a blue sweater and
black shoes. No tie need be worn when the sweater is on. The Head of School
is attired as befits a senior executive and all school prefects wear pin-striped
suits, collars and ties, brown or suede shoes. The boys are easy to talk to and
relations between different age groups are friendly. But their attitude is conservative, and innovations have to be persuasively sold to them. Religion is
applied in moderate doses. A service in the Abbey every Sunday and Wednesday is compulsory for the whole school, Juniors must attend a service in
the Victorian school chapel on Monday and Thursday, and there are
voluntary services for Seniors on Tuesday and Friday, the latter taken by
each House in turn. That this does not lead to religious indigestion is shown
by the good attendance – about 100 boys – at the voluntary communion
service held every Friday evening.

The decorum and conformism of Shirburnians may be due to the reassuring environment and distance from the corrupting delights of a big city. It
may also be due to the type of parents and the area they hail from. Geographically the catchment lies south of a crescent that curves from Exeter
through Stratford-upon-Avon to Hastings. The parents are overwhelmingly
from the tertiary economic class – the professions, service industries, armed
forces, law, commerce, banking. About 15 per cent of boys have an OS
father. Shirburnians when they leave mostly try for degree courses, over 80
per cent gaining places in 1984. Replies to a questionnaire sent to 175 OSs
who left in 1980 produced a 50 per cent response. Of the 80 who answered,
only 2 were not at a University or Polytechnic, 8 were going into commerce,
6 into business, 4 into a profession and 4 into the armed forces. At the University OSs have the reputation of doing well right through to Final exams,
not flopping to a low second class as some Award winners do.

Full School Service in Sherborne Abbey (*courtesy John Catt Ltd*)

The Shirburnian has a very well-balanced education, with a healthy mix of sports and work at a school which tries not to let the academic scene be dominated by exams. Control is not a great problem but is exercised with a caring as much as a policing attitude. Punishment is mostly by detention or imposing menial tasks. Beating by boys has disappeared and is used only rarely by Housemasters, though in extreme cases it is felt that beating is preferable to expulsion.

There are four examinations for entry, though most boys take Common Entrance. Contrary to rumour Sherborne has not raised the percentage required to pass, but some candidates have been advised that another school would suit them better. The school also runs its own exam for special cases, as well as its Scholarship exam for entry to the Lower School. There is also a special Scholarship for entry to the Sixth Form. Entries for both these Scholarships have been of a disappointing standard.

Sherborne has an unusual appendage in the shape of Greenhill House, at the top of the town. It is intended to provide a preparatory course for foreign boys and girls aged between 12 and 16 who wish to enter any British Public School. They undergo intensive teaching in English and share the amenities of the school. This is a somewhat lone endeavour in a field which the Public Schools might show more interest in. Many more foreign nationals would be glad to avail themselves of the unique opportunity of a boarding education in an English school, if they could only find the right channel of approach.

In 1982 the Sherborne Appeal was launched partly to fund various improvements and acquisitions, including the new Methodist Hall. Its main purpose was to provide more Scholarships of greater value to be awarded on academic merit, and Bursaries to help present Shirburnians whose families suffer unexpected financial loss. The Headmaster addressed meetings as far afield as Hong Kong, and when the Fund reached the original target of £700,000, the sights of the Appeal were raised to £1 million, so that the longer-term objectives could also be attained. Keeping up with the Etons in this competitive, technological age is expensive.

Sherborne School

ADDRESS Sherborne, Dorset DT9 3AP

FOUNDATION 8th century, refounded 1550 by King Edward VI

TITLE OF HEAD AND NUMBER OF TEACHING STAFF Headmaster + 72
(excluding visiting teachers)

TOTAL NUMBER OF PUPILS 650

NUMBER IN SIXTH FORM 205

NUMBER OF ADVANCED LEVEL CHOICES AVAILABLE 19

NAMES OF FORMS (i) Third (ii) Fourth (iii) Fifth (iv) Lower Sixth
(v) Upper Sixth

PRINCIPAL GAMES, BY TERMS *Michaelmas* Rugby *Lent* Hockey
Summer Cricket, Athletics, Tennis

NAMES OF HOUSES School House, Wallace House, The Digby, Abbey
House, Abbeylands, The Green, Lyon House, Harper House, Westcott
House

APPLICATION AND ENTRY Registration up to age 9 allows choice of House;
after age 9 the school allocates the House. Entry at 13+, or 16+ for Sixth
Form

SCHOLARSHIPS, ETC.
5 Open Scholarships of from 25% to 75% fees
2 Exhibitions for Officers in Armed Forces
3 Music Scholarships of from £600 to full fees
1 Art Scholarship of 25% fees

BOOK *A History of Sherborne School* by A.B. Gourlay

Winchester College

Scholars 70 BOARDING BOYS
Commoners 510 BOARDING BOYS
50 DAY BOYS

THE KING'S SCHOOL, CANTERBURY, CAN TRACE ITS ORIGINS BACK TO AD 600, but it was refounded by Henry VIII. Winchester, however, has occupied the same buildings without a break for 590 years. Its claim to be the first of those colleges which centuries later came to be known as Public Schools is beyond dispute.

In Saxon times Winchester was the capital of Wessex and therefore of England. It was here that King Arthur had his seat and there are grounds for believing that this was his fabled Camelot. Today it is largely a dormitory area, apart from its Law Courts, the barracks of the Greenjackets Regiment, the Cathedral and the College. The Cathedral stands between College and city. Its most famous bishop was Swithun, who died in 862. In his humility Swithun ordered that his body be buried outside the Cathedral. His command was broken on 15 July 971 when the grave was opened so that the Saint's remains could be transferred into the Cathedral. In protest the heavens wept copiously for forty days, and that is the origin of the legend that if it rains on St Swithun's Day it will rain for the next forty days. When the Cathedral was rebuilt in 1093 it became the largest in Europe after St Paul's, but it was the work done under Bishop William of Wykeham in the fourteenth century that brought about the most splendid transformation, combining height and length with dignity.

Wykeham was more than a bishop; he was also Chancellor of England (the equivalent of Prime Minister), a wealthy man and top of the executive class of his day. In 1380 he founded New College, Oxford to train the clerics needed to serve in a country devastated by the Black Death and shaken by the Peasants' Revolt. The walls surrounding New College and the castle-like Outer Gate of Winchester College are reminders of the turbulence of those times. Wykeham soon decided to found a school to prepare boys for his Oxford College. He purchased five acres of land south of the Cathedral from the Benedictine Priory of St Swithun's, and his school for 'poor scholars to the number of sixty and ten, studying in grammar' was opened in 1394. In 1984 Her Majesty the Queen was received in the traditional ceremony *ad portas* by the seventy Scholars, backed by more than five hundred Commoners. If you want to know why Winchester celebrated its Sexcentenary in

LEFT Chamber Court and Middle Gate (*photo David Herbert*)
RIGHT Way through from Chamber Court into School Court (*photo David Herbert*)

1984 when it had celebrated its Quincentenary in 1894, you'll have to ask one of the star Mathematicians for which the College is famous.

The most critical period in a long history was at the time of the English Reformation, when Henry VIII made himself Supreme Head of the Church in England, up-staging the Pope. But Winchester weathered his Act of Suppression and in 1547 'death stayed his rapacious hand'. In 1830 the College differed little from what it was in its mediaeval and monastic early days; living conditions were primitive and the Fellows prudently lived elsewhere, the boys still rose at 5.30 a.m. and did not breakfast till 10, and the teaching was concentrated on Latin. Gradually the tyranny of the prefects had become absolute and their instrument of rule was the ground-ash. In 1846 numbers had slumped from 140 to forty. The transference of power from the Warden and Fellows to the Headmaster enabled a succession of great Heads to reform the school, carry it through its Quingentenary and bring it triumphantly if prematurely to the celebrations of 1984.

Many of the buildings still in use today date from the original foundation, and are the subject of a brief guide longer than this chapter. Of outstanding interest are Outer Gate, Outer Court, Chamber Court, College Hall and the

The 17th-Century School, attributed to Wren (*photo David Herbert*)

Chapel. The roof of the latter is one of the first examples of a true fan vault, so notable a feature of the Perpendicular style, while the great East window and the 'misericord' seats are remarkable of their kind. Wykeham's Cloister is the resting place of Lord Wavell, the greatest of Wykehamist soldiers and also a scholar with a phenomenal memory for verse. Seventh Chamber, the original schoolroom, is the oldest in the land. The College was originally designed to house seventy Scholars, sixteen Quiristers and the ten permitted Commoners, plus about twenty staff. As more Commoners were admitted accommodation had to be extended. 'School' was built in 1683 to provide for the broadening of the Commoner entry and a far-sighted Headmaster, George Ridding, drained the land to the south and created the grassy swards of Meads for playing fields. Nine of the ten boarding Houses, residences in the nearest part of the town, were bought in the late nineteenth century. The Science block, built in 1904, marked the end of the dominance of Latin and was a bold step towards the age of Einstein. (He published his Relativity Theory in 1905, and eighty years later the implications of that astounding message have still hardly filtered into Science curricula.) New Hall, completed in 1960, foreshadowed the great upsurge of drama in Public Schools.

The War Cloister, commemorating the 770 Wykehamists killed in the two World Wars, is the most substantial such memorial in any school.

Winchester does not boast an ultra-modern Sports Hall nor a Design and Technology Centre bristling with computers and electronic equipment. Its boarding Houses have lagged behind the times and are only now being re-furbished and brought up to date. Yet a bigger proportion of this school's pupils win Awards to Cambridge and Oxford (and not only to New College) than any other. What are the factors that have led to this academic excellence?

The most important is the presence of seventy Scholars. In 1394 they constituted the entire school, in the mid-nineteenth century half the school, and by the 1980s they were outnumbered nine to one by Commoners. The scholarship examination, three days of intensive written tests, is of a very high standard, it is competitive and it attracts many of the brightest young boys in the country, many of whom are expertly coached for a place on the Winchester Election Roll. 'College men' live in the original buildings, where they are supervised by the Second Master, and headed by the majestic person of the Prefect of Hall. They still wear gowns for classes and formal occasions, they attend Preces (prayers) daily in Chapel and they eat in College Hall. A feature of life in College has long been the Chambers where the boys spend their days. There were five of them, each with about fourteen boys aged 13 to 18. Every boy had his own 'toy', one of the small semi-enclosed desk spaces round the room. In the middle was a big table and at the end an open fire. It is said that the mingling of older and younger boys made for tolerance and more rapid maturing, while the open plan encouraged a skill in discussion and debate which may account for the number of Wykehamists prominent in the Law. Recently a sixth Chamber has been opened to provide more space, College Men have bigger and more private toys and are more inclined to become Merchant Bankers. But the open fires in Chambers have survived.

The core of Scholars lifts the whole academic standard of the school as well as attracting the best qualified teachers. However, many who fail to get into College as Scholars are admitted to the school as Commoners, some with Exhibitions or Bursaries. Winchester differs from nearly all the Public Schools in not using the Common Entrance Examination. It sets its own test, largely because it does not regard CEE as a good exam. The subjects are much the same and the standard is not very much higher, but preparatory schools usually discourage less able boys from trying to get into Winchester. In fact selection is not on a competitive basis and is in the hands of the House-masters. They allocate places about two years before the entry date and the exam is taken at the age of 12 or 13. Houses contain about fifty boys and have meals under their own roofs. For the first two years Commoners have a 'toy' in a 'Mugging Hall', similar to a College Chamber, but thanks to the recent drive

OPPOSITE ABOVE The Royal Shrewsbury School Hunt (*W.G. Cross & Sons Ltd.*)
OPPOSITE BELOW Rugby School. View across the Close (*photo David Herbert*)

to improve Houses they now move up to studies and bed-sitters in their third year.

Every boy entering Winchester must realize that he is coming to a place where work is taken seriously and he will be competing with the very best. In many other ways the academic methods are different from other Public Schools, though they are becoming less so. The forms (called 'divisions') are in five groups: Junior Part, Middle Part, Transition Year (after O Level), Senior Part and Sixth Book. Termly promotion is possible, depending on individual ability and there is an internal examination every December. In Sixth Book and Senior Part there are three parallel ladders: A Ladder is Classical, B Ladder is Modern and C Ladder is Science, but boys often combine subjects from more than one Ladder. Up till now Ordinary Levels were not a static milestone which had to be passed at the end of, say, three years as in most schools. Boys took them in their stride according to their ability, some College Men even getting a few out of the way in their first year. The effect was not so much to enforce early specialization as to permit Dons (masters) to concentrate on Education in the fullest sense of the word. Classes could contain a mixture of boys aged 14 to 18 and the teaching would follow the Winchester syllabus rather than a GCE syllabus, Dons being given great freedom in teaching their subject.

As Winchester has attracted some of the most inspiring and eccentric teachers the value of this freedom was incalculable. Many Dons have pioneered A level courses now used generally. Just recently the importance of Ordinary Levels for purposes of University entrance has led to a change in this flexible approach. Now only the Mathematics department follows the old usage. Mathematics was for long the *second* most important subject and has now become *the* most important, over half of Sixth Book (Sixth Form) studying the subject. So the department had the strength to resist the change. Though the supremacy of the Classics was broken in 1901, Latin is still compulsory in the Lower school. Until 1960 no Science was taught in the Lower school, though now it takes up a quarter of the timetable for the first two years. Modern Languages have been taught for 160 years but the English department has only been in existence for eighteen years, because English, like History and Divinity, was taught in 'Div'.

'Div' is a special feature which runs right up through the school. Every boy has six periods a week with his 'Div Don', who can choose what to do with his class. In the Lower school certain subjects have to be covered but apart from that there is no syllabus, a Don may communicate his own interests and enthusiasm to his div, doing anything from Wagner's 'Ring' to the works of Fritjov Capra. In Winchester this takes the place of General Studies and mitigates over-specialization. Equally important in Sixth Book are 'task-times', which boys have every week with the Dons teaching their main subjects. Then, on a person-to-person basis, some piece of work done by the pupil is discussed in depth. Some Dons regard this as the most valuable educational exercise of all.

Winchester College Football on College Meads (*photo David Herbert*)

Sixth Formers have a liberal allowance of 'books chambers', periods for
private study in their own rooms or 'toys'. Lights-out rules are often lenient
so that older boys may in practice work on into the small hours, or rise with
the birds. In College there are only a few hours in the dead of night when all
are asleep.

The result of this system is that it is very rare indeed for a Wykehamist to
fail at Ordinary Level. At Advanced Level the pass rate is generally not far
short of 100 per cent, and in 1984 in twelve of the twenty subjects taken *all*
candidates passed. The figure of Grade A's obtained was 44 per cent, while
in the S (Scholarship) papers taken Grades 1 and 2 were achieved by 21.5 per
cent. The table of Oxford and Cambridge Awards in *The Times Educational
Supplement* of 27 May 1984 showed that Winchester had won twenty-seven,
the highest proportion of any school in relation to the size of the Sixth Form
(297).

The Outer Gate of College has some of the defensiveness of a fortress and
it has been said, unfairly, that Winchester is an inward-looking place, dis-
trustful of outsiders and prone to intellectual arrogance. This impression is
reinforced by the difficulty of gaining entry, academically speaking, as well as
by the mystique of its academic life and its private language, called Notions.
The largest guide to Notions ever printed ran to 1,000 words, the current
booklet lists 200. It still contains some picturesque terminology: man (boy in
the school), mugging (school work), quill (source of pleasure), pussy (woollen
scarf), toytime (evening prep), hot (scrimmage), Lords (1st XI) and Morning Hills.

This last refers to the custom of the whole school trekking up to the top of
nearby St Catherine's Hill, which was once the playing field, on the first

morning of Cloister Time and Short Half (Summer and Autumn terms). The First Cricket Eleven is still called Lords, though Winchester has not played on the MCC ground since 1854. Win Co Fu is a special brand of football played in Common Time (Spring term) with rules and terminology too complex to describe here. *Ad portas*, the ceremony when a distinguished visitor is welcomed with a Latin speech from the Prefect of College, recently marked the arrival of ten High Court Judges, all of them Wykehamists. *Illumina* is a ceremony on the last night of Short Half when Meads is illuminated by a bonfire and candles placed in 'temples' – the Notion for niches in the surrounding walls – themselves built of stone from an ancient convent. Winchester is probably the only school whose song expresses nostalgia for home, a doleful chant entitled *Dulce Domun*. The top hat vanished long ago, and now the strat (straw hat) has followed it. College Men may still wear gowns but the dress of Commoners is informal though tidy, with grey suits on Sundays.

It is true that the College has provided many eminent men of Law, but the Wykehamist 'type' is found more in fiction than reality. Wykehamists, and especially Collegemen, are inevitably of above average intelligence, but they are on the whole tolerant, and generous in the use of their intellectual gifts. Not many are drawn to politics and Winchester has provided only one rather insignificant Prime Minister, Henry Addington. There have been just two Wykehamists in every Parliament since 1966. Cripps, Crossman and Gaitskell have given the College a reputation for being Socialist, but in fact

Chapel, with School on the right and Flint Court between two wings of the classrooms on the left (*photo David Herbert*)

Wykehamists are predominantly Conservative. In the world of Art they tend to be critics rather than creators, though Sir Kenneth Clark raised criticism to the level of an art. There have been innumerable academics of distinction, including the Headmaster elect, himself a Wykehamist and at the time of writing a Don in the school. Leavers in the years 1965 to 1980 have become Chairmen of well over a hundred companies, and one of them, Sir Denys Lowson, was the youngest ever Lord Mayor of London. It was a Wykehamist, Richard Noble, who recovered the world's land speed record with his Thrust 2, and next time you watch a Test batsman duck under a bouncer remember that it was Wykehamist Douglas Jardine who, as the England cricket skipper, first introduced body-line bowling.

Winchester College

ADDRESS Winchester, Hampshire SO23 9LX

FOUNDATION 1382 by William of Wykeham, Bishop of Winchester

GOVERNING BODY Warden and 12 Fellows

TITLE OF HEAD AND NUMBER OF TEACHING STAFF Headmaster + 82 (excluding visiting teachers)

TOTAL NUMBER OF PUPILS 630

NUMBER OF SIXTH FORM 390

NUMBER OF ADVANCED LEVEL CHOICES AVAILABLE 15+

NAMES OF FORMS (i) Junior Part (ii) Middle Part (iii) Transition Year (iv) Senior Part (v) VIth Book

PRINCIPAL GAMES, BY TERMS *Short Half* Soccer *Common Time* Winchester Football *Cloister Time* Cricket and Rowing

NAMES OF HOUSES College and 10, named A to K: A Chernocke House; B Moberly's; C Du Boulay; D Fearon's; E Morshead's; F Hawkins'; G Sergeant's; H Bramston's; I Turner's; K Kingsgate House.

APPLICATION AND ENTRY Commoners apply to a Housemaster at age 8+. Entry at age 12–14; Scholars by competitive examination, Commoners by a qualifying Winchester examination.

SCHOLARSHIPS
2 Major Scholarships of 100% of fees
About 15 Scholarships of 60% of fees
About 6 Exhibitions of up to 30% of fees
plus 5 Assisted Places
3 Music Exhibitions of £2,505+

BOOK *Winchester College* by James Sabben-Clare.

Shrewsbury School

SHREWSBURY WAS ONE OF THE SACRED SEVEN COVERED BY THE PUB-lic Schools Act of 1869, an honour which it shared with Charterhouse, Eton, Harrow, Rugby, Westminster and Winchester. Rugby owed its fame to Dr Arnold; Shrewsbury's was built up by a triumvirate of great headmasters. Their consecutive reigns lasted 110 years and between them they took the school from the eighteenth to the twentieth century.

The school had been founded in 1552 by Royal Charter. Edward VI's government used at least some of the money pillaged from dissolved religious institutions to found such schools. The term *Libera Schola Grammaticalis* meant that it was free from church control, not free gratis and for nothing. Fees have always been payable, for the Shrewsbury 'Schools' were not lavishly endowed. The first Master, Thomas Ashton, hob-nobbed with the greatest in the land. By 1562 he had 266 boys and by 1586 his was the biggest school in England. One of his pupils was Sir Philip Sidney, but that did not prevent the school entering a period of decline and obscurity which lasted till the end of the eighteenth century.

When Samuel Butler was appointed in 1798, he took over a school of less than twenty boys. Within a few years he had raised the number to 295. Well before Arnold he fostered a prefectorial system and strove to turn out boys who were 'good Christians, good scholars, and honourable and useful members of society'. He was the first schoolmaster in England to become famous purely because of his brilliance as a teacher. He taught the Fifth and Sixth Forms, a total of 120 boys, with astonishing success. In Cambridge his pupils won 16 Browne Medals, 9 Chancellor's Medals, 19 University Scholarships and 11 Porson Prizes, often while still at school. His reputation as a flogging headmaster is unfair. 'The punishment,' he wrote, 'is one which I hold best for little boys and worst for big ones.' His regime survived the 'epidemic of turbulence' that hit Public Schools in 1818. In 1821 he introduced Speech Days, when the Speeches were given by the boys, as at Eton today, and it was he who brought in a system of internal examinations, which was later adopted by Eton and Harrow.

He was succeeded by one of his own pupils, Benjamin Hall Kennedy, 'the greatest classical teacher of the century'. His pupils won even more prizes than Butler's. The desk on which he wrote his *Shorter Latin Primer*, all too well known to millions of schoolboys, is still used by today's Headmaster. The next Master, Henry Whitehead Moss, was appointed in 1866, aged 25. Amazingly, he ran the school without a secretary or bursar and also took the whole work of the Sixth. In modern times nine people have been needed to do the work that he shouldered. From the start he was convinced that the Schools – Lower, Middle and Upper – had to be moved out of Shrewsbury town. His view prevailed, and in 1882 he transferred 160 boys to the present site on land called Kingsland, where there was a large Common and a capacious building. The House of Industry (a euphemism for Workhouse) was purchased and adapted by the architect Blomfield as a classroom block. Next door Moss built School House, where a hundred boarders could be accommodated. During succeeding years the school purchased land and houses as they became available, extending southwards till it now covers 105 acres, largely of green sward.

In the twentieth century Shrewsbury marked time longer than most Public Schools. Not till 1963 was it made aware, sometimes painfully, that the world was changing, but during the twelve years of Donald Wright's Headmastership the place altered drastically and for a time got ahead of the field. Up till then 80 per cent of the best intellects traditionally opted for

The main school building, formerly the House of Industry (*Shrewsbury School*)

Classics. Now choice replaced compulsion and as many chose Science and Maths as the Humanities. In games as well the options were widened. The old hierarchical boy privileges wasted away, relationships between older and younger boys became less formal, teachers forsook gown and mortar-board and came down off their dais to be on a level with their class. Compulsory Chapel every day and twice on Sunday gave way to one service in the week and one on Sunday. The school became more relaxed, more friendly.

Shrewsbury's 105 acres of upland are south of the almost complete circle which the River Severn describes round the town. The Shropshire Hills are visible to the west and Wales is only eight miles away. The A5 runs past to the south and when you turn off it up the hill you burst suddenly onto this broad, open and spacious site with its vast Common in the middle of a semi-circle of brick buildings round the perimeter, and over it all 'the sky's unresting cloudland'. The character of the school is shaped by its site, for it is dispersed yet unified, a society that reflects from many facets. There being no central quadrangle or hub, the community divides naturally into its different groups and the reins of control are held lightly. Access to the central playing fields is easy, the river is about three minutes from the boarding Houses and the open country is on the southern doorstep. To the tradition of scholarship that Moss brought from the old Schools has been added a great reputation for games. Shrewsbury has the advantage that the Common is private. No road runs through it, it is not overlooked. This allows a more informal posture without the danger of criticism from outsiders. Gone are the mortar-boards and top hats worn in Moss's day. The boys – there are no girls here – wear grey flannels, a jacket or blazer, white shirt, collar and tie. A tendency to wear the neck undone and to return to school with dyed hair has been checked.

In 1974 the building of a central eating place, Kingsland Hall, lessened the privacy of the boarding Houses and their Housemasters. The whole school now came together three times a day for a non-ritualistic gathering. Houses still sat separately but divided by a mystical rather than physical partition. The new Science Laboratories, a single-storey building, reflect the shift away from the Classics. Well-planned and up-to-date, they house a youthful department. The seventeen Science teachers each have a combined laboratory cum classroom and normally teach 28 out of the 36 weekly periods. The Charles Darwin Museum is an ironic reminder that Darwin studied not Science but Classics and Theology at Shrewsbury. The Computer Room, open to all from 7 a.m. till 10 p.m. daily, has twelve terminals linked to the school's ICL 2903 computer, thus giving free access to a vast range of programs, and ample disc storage space. The new Electronics Room will develop and take shape as this book is being printed. First year boys spend two weeks of Maths time in the computer department, second year boys give twenty periods of Physics time to micro-electronics, robotics and digital electronics, while one tenth of the Advanced Level Physics course is on electronics.

The old Science building has now become the Art School, offering generous space to a subject which is growing. In 1984 twelve boys were doing Art at Advanced Level. Encouragement has been given to Drama by the conversion of the old Gym to a modern theatre seating 250 with sophisticated lighting controlled by computer. It was opened by the actor Robert Hardy (son of a former Headmaster) in 1984. The new Gym with its brick casing looms over the Common from an abutment that used to be called the Pier, and emphasizes the diversity of games now available, complementing the old Eton fives courts and the new squash courts. Tudor Court is a new club for older boys, where they have a bar run by themselves and to which they can invite girl friends from the town or nearby schools. Tudor Court also contains study–bedroom accommodation for Upper Sixth boys. A master, the Warden, keeps an eye on all this. The Craft Centre provided the incentive for four boys who built an electric invalid car which won the BP Young Engineer of Britain prize. By contrast, the Moser Library, now world famous, has an importance out of all proportion to its size. It possesses seventy-three incunabula including the finest copy of John Gower's *Confessio Amantis* printed by Caxton in 1483, as well as every type of binding from the fifteenth century onwards.

Of the old buildings the Chapel (a Gothic revival building by Blomfield in his least inspired mood), Alington Hall and the old Schools remain largely unchanged. The boarding Houses have been modernized. Of these only Oldham's Hall, Neville Shute's old House, was purpose-built. The rest are mansions bought by the school, then converted and extended. Most accommodate about sixty boys, though Dayboys House has 115 and School House ninety-two. The latter is theoretically divided into 'Doctor's' and 'Headroom', to prevent it winning all the competitions, but is still run by one intrepid Housemaster. Housemasters are free to allocate accommodation as they wish. There are some bed-sitters for seniors but most boys sleep in bedrooms (the word dormitory is not used here) and share studies. Some Housemasters mix the age groups, some group them by seniority, others let the boys arrange things among themselves. It is all very flexible, in the typical Salopian fashion. (Salopian is derived from the Saxon Salopscire – whence 'Shropshire'.)

Housemasters, who supervise a boy's activities throughout his years at the school, have the assistance of one resident and perhaps four non-resident Tutors. For his first three years a boy's work is supervised by his Form Master, and he is kept up to the mark by fortnightly report cards and a half-term report. Entering the Sixth Form he chooses a master who will be his academic Tutor and give him general help and guidance. Here the well-tried teaching methods are regarded as best, and modern ideas are only brought in as common sense dictates. Masters take turns to teach the lowest and the highest classes, thus emphasizing that the plodder gets as much attention as the high-flyer. This results in a good overall performance in GCE, with over 90 per cent of candidates passing both O and A Levels.

Aerial view of Kingsland with River Severn and town in the background (© *Aerofilms Ltd*)

Now that Awards to Cambridge and Oxford have come to an end, Shrewsbury can look back on its record of 592 won from 1920 to 1984, with eight won in 1984. The shift of emphasis shows up in a comparison of Classics and Science/Maths achievements:

	1920–29	1970–79
Classics	74	14
Maths/Science	14	42

Shrewsbury has pioneered activities which do not show in the academic results tables, especially in the field of industrial relations. A head-

The School Regatta on Speech Day (*Shrewsbury School*)

line in *The Times* in 1978 proclaimed 'Small hurricane at Shrewsbury. Many myths dead.' It referred to the Careers Master's initiative in bringing masters as well as boys together with senior businessmen for a Challenge of Management Conference. An outcome of this has been the Pre-University Industrial Experience Scheme (INDEX) available to all schools, maintained and independent.

Easy access to the Common and the River Severn have fostered a strong tradition in rowing, cricket and association football. It was a Salopian, J.C. Thring, who was instrumental in drafting the 1862 'Rules of the Simplest Game' which were accepted by the Football Association. In 1927 the Oxford boat race crew came up to be coached by a master here. The Hunt claims to be the oldest cross-country running club in the world. There is no live quarry, the 'hounds' are younger boys, the 'gentlemen' older ones; there are a Huntsman and Whips with appropriate livery, and the purpose is not so much to race as to run, in a 'Chariots of Fire' spirit. There are regular courses such as the Bog or the Biggin and the winner is said to have 'killed'. Is this the most humane form of blood sport?

The Salopian of today is informal but not scruffy. He has a lot of personal freedom and is quite happy without girls in the school. There are girls in the day schools nearby whom he can meet for drama or music or at discos, as well as girls in the town where he is allowed to go freely. Nowadays he is less likely to turn up and cheer for a school team than to go off in pursuit of his own interests. He is easy to meet but perhaps a little cloistered. A master's wife, comparing Salopians with their contemporaries at a maintained day school, commented that they were 'more confident but less mature'. They have abandoned tedious and oppressive traditions, no longer carve their names on the massive stone blocks brought up from the old Schools. But some of the old terminology is preserved. House prayers are 'Dix', prep is 'Top Schools', festive events are 'Fasti', and the school Praeposters still carry knobbed canes on Speech Day.

With 110 day boys and 550 boarders Shrewsbury is a local as well as a national school. The catchment area for Salopian boarders has shrunk in the last few decades and is now concentrated more in the traditional areas – the Wirral, Lancashire, Cheshire, Yorkshire and the industrial Midlands. About a third of the parents are from industry and commerce, another third from the professions. About 20 per cent of fathers are Salopians and 40 per cent are non-Public School men. The preponderance of grass roots farmers and industrialists makes for a healthy mix and there is no uniform accent. These parents are making a calculated investment and want to know that they are getting value for money. It is noticeable that there are few from Birmingham, which has such excellent day schools.

Shrewsbury's most distinguished alumni in the past were Sidney and Darwin and she can parade an array of figures prominent in today's public life. Reading from right to left we can identify Lord Lane (Lord Chief Justice), Michael Heseltine, Richard Ingrams, William Rushton, Paul Foot.

(*Sutherland Hawes Design*)

Shrewsbury School

ADDRESS Shrewsbury, Shropshire SY3 7BA

FOUNDATION 1552 by King Edward VI

TITLE OF HEAD AND NUMBER OF TEACHING STAFF Headmaster + 67 (excluding visiting teachers)

TOTAL NUMBER OF PUPILS 665

NUMBER IN SIXTH FORM 260

NUMBER OF ADVANCED LEVEL CHOICES AVAILABLE 19

NAMES OF FORMS (i) Fourth (ii) Fifth (iii) Remove (iv) Lower Sixth (v) Middle Sixth (vi) Upper Sixth

PRINCIPAL GAMES, BY TERMS *Autumn* Soccer *Spring* Cross-Country, Rugby and Rowing *Summer* Cricket and Rowing

NAMES OF HOUSES
Boarding The School House ('Headroom' and 'Doctor's'), Rigg's Hall, Churchill's Hall, Moser's Hall, Severn Hill, Ingram's Hall, Oldham's Hall, Ridgemount
Day Port Hill, Radbrook

APPLICATION AND ENTRY Registration any time up to year of entry, with choice of House. Entry at 13+ and 16+.

SCHOLARSHIPS, ETC.
4 Scholarships of 50% of fees
4 Scholarships of 33% of fees
2 Scholarships of 25% of fees
7 Exhibitions of £450 p.a.
2 Junior Scholarships for boys of 10+ (2 years at preparatory school and 5 years at Shrewsbury)
2 Scholarships for Sixth Form entry
4 Music Scholarships of up to 50% of fees

TOTAL ANNUAL ALLOCATION FOR SCHOLARSHIPS, ETC. £193,946

BOOK *A History of Shrewsbury School* by Basil Oldham

Rugby School

636 BOARDING BOYS

65 DAY BOYS

37 BOARDING GIRLS

12 DAY GIRLS

RUGBY LIES AT THE VERY CENTRE OF ENGLAND, EMBRACED BY THREE motorways – M1, M6 and M45 – which have replaced the train in making the school accessible to an extensive catchment area. From the time of the Industrial Revolution it has been well placed to pull in the sons of the newly prosperous middle-class, solid, reliable North-country people. There has always been a leavening of Londoners, and in the 1980s a generous sprinkling from Hong Kong.

Rugby was founded in 1567 by Lawrence Sheriff. He had been born in the town but moved to London, where he became prominent in the Grocers' Company. His Will provided for a School and Almshouses to meet the needs of his birthplace; and by a happy after-thought he added a codicil leaving the school an obscure place called Conduit Close. When London expanded it became Conduit Street in Mayfair, and this windfall was what allowed Rugby to become a great school. It enabled the trustees, 'twelve gentlemen of Warwickshire', to move the school to its present site. Numbers rose to 300. The customary rebellion in 1797 against excessive beating was put down by excessive beating, but the school survived and even prospered, waiting for the fourteen-year reign of Dr Thomas Arnold, 1828–42.

Arnold's shadow looms large over Rugby. His great contribution was that he put an end to the savage conditions which had prevailed in such schools. He made the Public School respectable, a place in whose bosom parents could comfortably put their sons. His declared object was 'the creation of Christian gentlemen', and he used a prefectorial system to achieve this end, as Shrewsbury's Samuel Butler had done before him. But it was he who set up the House system, gave his Housemasters independence and emphasized their pastoral role. His emphasis on religion has sometimes been described as 'muscular Christianity', but Arnold did not see games as an aid to moulding the character of boys. He was a reformer in 'cleansing the Temple' of the Public School, but he was conservative where the curriculum was concerned. He was, of course, a brilliant Classicist. For him Latin and Greek were the basis of education and he made the teaching of Science virtually impossible. Thomas Hughes' novel *Tom Brown's Schooldays* fixed both Arnold and Public Schools in the popular mind. Lytton Strachey satirized him but not till Macdonald Fraser wrote his Flashman novels was the image tarnished.

In fact, it was because games were subject to no control or rules that a boy picked up the football and ran with it in his hands. So here in 1845 appeared the first Rules of Rugby Football and pilgrims still come to see the little Rugby Football Museum in the library, and the Close where our last great amateur sport was born.

Arnold's ashes lie under a plain black cross-shaped stone in the Chapel. One wonders whether Rugby has ever quite recovered from the days when a flag flew from the School House mast to show that 'the Doctor' was in his study and available to boys. Since then being Head Master has never been an easy task.

The school's magnetic centre is the Old Quad, a somewhat gloomy enclave flanked by the archaic School House. On one side a gate leads straight out onto the streets of the Town. On the other a square tunnel leads to New Quad and the Chapel, designed by Butterfield in 1872. It contains interesting stained glass, including a fifteenth-century Flemish window, bought by Dr Arnold. Butterfield also designed the New Quad classrooms, New Big Schools and the Temple Library. Dr Frederick Temple, Head Master from 1858–69, was in the Rugby mould of high-minded left-wing intellectualism. He became Archbishop of Canterbury and thus rated another memorial, the Temple Speech Room. The new theatre, in an old building, is equipped with every technical device and is in regular use for House plays.

When you pass through Old Quad and emerge onto the Close, a historic expanse of green sward, you see on your left what looks like a small township, of mostly brick buildings. The buildings extend down the busy Barby Road towards Spring Hill playing fields. Some are masters' residences and class-rooms but mostly they are the Houses, regarded as so important by Arnold. Today the House is still the focal point of a pupil's existence. The twelve Houses are separate identities, and their independence is reinforced by the fact that there is no central feeding. Each House sits down to meals in its own dining-room, presided over by the Matron, Housemaster and perhaps his

The Dowager Queen Adelaide with Matthew and Thomas Arnold watching an early game of rugger. Painting by Jane Arnold 1839 (*photo Geoffrey Creighton Studio*)

wife. Inter-house team games to decide which House shall be Cock House are the life-blood of the school. Houses number up to seventy, enough to field several teams. Younger boys and those less expert at sports play most of their games on a House basis and each House has its own quad for informal cricket or football. Although games no longer dominate school life as they did, to be given your 'bags' (be named as one of the best Rugger players in the school) is still a distinction to be proud of.

The Housemaster is of course the most important person in a boy's life. He has the assistance of a non-resident Tutor and his wife is often an unpaid helper. Living conditions are becoming less spartan as the Houses are modernized; the last old-style dormitory with wash basins down the middle (Upper Big) and adjoining bathrooms with the famous 'toshes' disappeared in 1985. (The name was a contraction of 'to wash' and described a round tub in which only the middle of the body could be submerged.) There are few study–bedrooms. Boarding boys sleep in partly partitioned dormitories, in high beds with 'coffins' under them. At the end of his time a Sixth (Prefect) goes back to take charge of a junior dorm, his bed distinguished by a brown blankct. In the daytime boys share a study for the first three years, and after O Level they have a single study. Fagging still survives, but it is on a voluntary basis, when 'Sixths' arrange for a junior boy to do jobs for them. As they get paid for this, the juniors are quite happy to oblige.

School House, with many more boys than other Houses, is historically something of a House apart. In Dr Arnold's day the rest of the school played Rugger against School House, with many more than fifteen players a side. Until recently the Head Master was its Housemaster; S.H. boys used to refer to him by his Christian name, though to others he was The Bodger. The last of the School House 'toshes' vanished some time ago and a new dining room has been constructed alongside the hall where Tom Brown was 'roasted' by Flashman. The tiny but private studies remain and most inmates are as proud of them as of the other traditions of the House.

'Dropping the Island Goal' by C.H. Chambers *c.*1846 (*photo Geoffrey Creighton Studio*)

Town House is for day boys, of which there are sixty-five. Its facilities are much the same as in boarding Houses, though of course there are no dormitories. Dean, Crescent and Southfield are the girls' Houses, where day girls and boarders enjoy Sixth Form College conditions under the supervision of a Housemaster and his wife. In their first year girl boarders share a bed-sitter and in the second have one to themselves. They have a cheerful common-room with cooking equipment, TV and Hi-fi where they can socialize and invite boy-friends. Boys are not allowed past the door that leads to their private quarters, and if a boy hangs about in a tiresome manner they find ways of letting him know he is not wanted. Together the girls create a strong community spirit. Each one is attached to a boys' House for lunch and tea plus other shared activities. There are usually over fifty applicants for the available places. As most of those selected are potential Cambridge and Oxford material, they form an elite element in the Sixth Form. In fact the girls plus the day boys produce half the Grade A Advanced Levels won by Rugby, and of course they account for a high proportion of the places won at the two major Universities. Rugbeians won nine Awards to Cambridge and Oxford in 1983–4. The performance at Advanced Level remains a mystery, as Rugby, in common with a few other schools, declined to disclose its GCE results to the author of a book.

The girls are one change that would have surprised a Dr Arnold returning

Temple Reading Room and Statue of Thomas Hughes, author of *Tom Brown's Schooldays*, by John Shakespeare (*Rugby School*)

from the past. He would, of course, grieve at the nation's decline in moral standards but be reassured by the five compulsory Chapel attendances per week. He might feel that the Christian spirit is more truly expressed in the community work which takes a hundred boys into the town in their third year. Boys are no longer 'moulded', he would note, for individuality is now encouraged. The Eton jacket and collar have given way to a tweed jacket, grey flannels, white shirt and House tie. And (publish it not in the streets of Askelon) boys are allowed to wear jeans to go into the town so as not to provoke a Town v Gown confrontation. The theatre is no longer sinful, for over twenty productions a year take place annually, most of them House plays in the modern theatre inserted into New Big School. But Arnold's classical mind would be most discountenanced by the changes in the curriculum. He might protest at boys doing up to fourteen subjects for O Level and then narrowing down to only three for A Level, protest at the tyranny of this external taskmaster, which makes the young mind dig in behind a restricted perimeter of approved facts instead of reaching out to embrace wider horizons of knowledge; though he would note with pleasure that all pupils in the Upper School are required to spend a third of their class time doing non-examinable subjects; four periods a week on 'Themes' (a common core course), three on 'Electives' (literary, practical or artistic) and four on a wide variety of Options. Greek and Latin are still studied for Advanced Level. Now *all* boys do three Science subjects up to O Level, and *half* the pupils choose to do some Science in the Sixth Form!

Actually Rugby pioneered the first Science lectures in a school, in 1740. Arnold quenched Science, but it was rekindled later. The first regular Science teacher was appointed in 1851 and in 1864 it became a compulsory subject. Science Schools were built in 1903, superseded in 1971 and extended in 1982, when computing and electronics were incorporated in the Rugby Science course. A Rugby master, Mr G.E. Foxcroft, received an OBE for his part in the development of Nuffield Science. Science took its chance in the late 1960s. At many schools, when the Classics declined, Geography and History stepped in, but here Science established itself as a major academic discipline, and in the last thirty years the number doing Science has risen from 10.6 per cent to 26 per cent. The emphasis is on learning techniques and discovery rather than memorizing for regurgitation. The subject is taught for fun rather than for GCE exams, and if the exam is not right the Board is persuaded to change it. The Science Department has its own separate budget and gets from the Governors more or less what it asks for, so it is not surprising if the equipment is lavish. In the Common Entrance exam Rugby regards Science as a supporting subject, but in the Scholarship exam it is compulsory. In 1983 50 per cent of those who got places at Cambridge and Oxford offered a Maths or Science subject. And, interestingly, pupils are going up to do Law or English at Cambridge having done A Levels in Maths, Physics and Chemistry.

Today's Rugbeian does not spare too many thoughts for the Doctor, nor

Outside Chapel (*photo Paul Martin*)

for Rugby worthies of the past. Arnold's pupils became Headmasters of at least fourteen other schools, though Robert Birley, Head Master of Eton, was of a later generation. The boy of today is probably more aware of the Rugby poets – Rupert Brooke, Walter Savage Landor, Matthew Arnold, Arthur Hugh Clough – or of Lewis Carrol, the creator of *Alice in Wonderland*, and the contemporary novelist Salman Rushdie; and perhaps also of Arthur Bliss, who foreshadowed the strong musical emphasis that has been such an inspirational element in the School's life since his day. Such names counteract the saying that Rugby produces safe and worthy but not very exciting *alumni*.

It is justifiably regarded as one of *the* leading schools, with many important features not mentioned in this brief account – the gigantic open-air swimming pool, the War Memorial Chapel, the wide Close, the copper beeches and cedars of Lebanon, the spring blossom.

Rugbeians are not wedded to tradition, though it surrounds them, and some of it survives. At the end of the Lent Term most boys and some girls take part in the Crick, a cross-country race of $10\frac{1}{2}$ miles. The Levee, that august body of school Prefects, now includes a couple of girls. But the Head of School does not exercise his ancient right to possess a carriage, a house in the town, a wife, two children and a dog.

Rugby School

ADDRESS Rugby, Warwickshire CV22 5EH

FOUNDATION 1567 by Lawrence Sheriff

TITLE OF HEAD AND NUMBER OF TEACHING STAFF Head Master + 84
(excluding visiting teachers)

TOTAL NUMBER OF PUPILS 770

NUMBER IN SIXTH FORM 350

NUMBER OF ADVANCED LEVEL CHOICES AVAILABLE 21

NAMES OF FORMS (i) F Block (ii) E Block (iii) D Block (iv) Lower Twenty
(v) The Twenty (vi) Sixth Form

PRINCIPAL GAMES, BY TERMS *Advent* Rugby *Lent* Hockey *Trinity* Cricket
and Athletics

NAMES OF HOUSES
Boarding boys School, Bradley, Sheriff, Stanley, School Field, Whitelaw,
Michell, Tudor, Kilbracken, Cotton
Day boys Town
Boarding girls Dean, Southfield, Crescent
Day girls Crescent

APPLICATION AND ENTRY Application via Head Master or a Housemaster.
Entry for boys at 13+ any term, girls 15–16+ Advent term

SCHOLARSHIPS, ETC.
Town House
14 Major Scholarships of 100% tuition fees
21 Minor Scholarships of 50% tuition fees

Boarding Houses
2 Scholarships of 80% full fees
1 Scholarship of 60% full fees
1 Scholarship of 50% full fees
2 Scholarships of 35% full fees
6 Scholarships of 15% full fees
3 Music Scholarships of 75%, 60% and 40% full fees
1 Art Scholarship of £500 p.a.
(All the above, except the Art Scholarship, may be augmented to
100% full fees)

TOTAL ANNUAL ALLOCATION FOR SCHOLARSHIPS, ETC. £100,000 not
counting augmentation

BOOK *Rugby School* by J.B. Hope Simpson

Uppingham School

563 BOARDING BOYS

12 DAY BOYS

50 BOARDING GIRLS

10 DAY GIRLS

UPPINGHAM IS AN ATTRACTIVE OLD MARKET TOWN IN THE UN-spoilt country of Rutland, and is twinned with Caudebec-en-Cau in Normandy. The school, which is twinned with Oakham ten miles to the north, forms part of the town and stretches westward along the ridge of a plateau. The boarding Houses are scattered to north, east and west of the central cluster of small, friendly courts and quadrangles. The locally quarried grey and russet ironstone gives a unity of tone and texture to buildings of varied periods and style. The countryside and green fields are a few minutes' walk away so it does not take long to get to the playing fields – sixty acres of them, graced by two thatched pavilions.

Uppingham, like Oakham, was founded in 1584 by Robert Johnson, an Elizabethan worthy, who had the gift that 'he could surprise a miser into charity'. He raised enough money – and perhaps this was the first Appeal – to found two schools and two hospitals or almshouses, obtaining letters patent from Queen Elizabeth I. Uppingham's history came to life in 1853, when Edward Thring was appointed Headmaster, eleven years after Dr Arnold had retired from Rugby. Thring had been educated in College at Eton, where conditions were notoriously tough, and was resolved to human-ize boarding-school life. Public schoolboys probably owe more to him than to any other reformer. If Arnold moulded character, Thring encouraged individuality. To him small was beautiful, and when numbers in the school grew from a dozen to 300 he called a halt. He encouraged masters to buy boarding Houses and run them with a pastoral emphasis, he had partitions put round the beds in dormitories to give some privacy, and he saw that every boy had a study or part of a study to work in. To break routine, which he hated, he introduced non-academic activities – music, art, crafts, as well as organized games. He raised eyebrows by his eagerness to take his coat off and join in the team games of his pupils. Though the Classics still held pride of place in the curriculum he was concerned primarily with the development in his pupils of body, mind and spirit – the hallmark of the true educator. He had little patience with bureaucracy. When the local water supply was found to be contaminated he decamped with the whole school to Borth on the Welsh coast till the local authority had put the matter right. That event is still remembered in an annual Chapel service. He founded the Head

Masters' Conference in 1869 and when he died in 1887 he was still in harness.

Standing in what was Dr Thring's study at one end of the Memorial Library one senses the man's presence, and this may not be an illusion for it is his influence that makes Uppingham the stimulating, sympathetic community it is now. His ideas on the education of the whole man (person) are propounded today in radical teacher training colleges – but not attributed to a Victorian Public School Headmaster.

Thring appointed as music director a Herr Paul David, whose father in Leipzig was a friend of Mendelssohn. He held the post from 1864 to 1910 and established a strong tradition of music. In the Paul David Theatre the famous violinist Joaquim gave his last performance of Beethoven's Violin Concerto. Now, some 300 pupils learn a musical instrument and four are currently taking A Level Music. The whole school sings lustily in Chapel and 250 take part in such performances as the St Matthew Passion. An LP, produced by Uppingham School Choirs 1980–82, is evidence of the extent to which Music Scholarships have raised the standard. Many pupils have later become academic or professional musicians. In the last decade ten have won organ or choral Awards at University. The House Shout is as keenly contested as House rugger and produces anything from Verdi to Presley. It can be revealed without shame that a team returning from an away match were heard singing the Hallelujah Chorus! A fine new Music School presents a low profile from the quadrangle, its three storeys being absorbed by the slope of the hill. On the top storey is the Buttery, to which the strains of Allegri's setting of the 51st Psalm may waft up from a music class below.

The Thring Centre, opened in 1965, recalls that Headmaster's insistence on providing a diversity of activities to meet all tastes. It is a former manor house where now, for instance, ceramics, woodwork, camera and TV work are available. The Art School proper is in the original Elizabethan School House under the shadow of the Parish Church. This was one of the first schools to appoint a professional art master, who took the title Director of Technique and Vision. He pioneered Design as an A Level subject and persuaded the Board to set a paper. That seed has born fruit, for in 1984 about 150 OUs in design-orientated professions provided material for an exhibition in Glaziers Hall. Here too was created the design for the extension of the Chapel in 1965, so that it would seat the whole school. It is an imaginative concept, one whole wall swung back like an opened glass door through which light and colour stream in from Chapel Lawn. The cost of £75,000 was produced by one donor, thanks to a chance remark made by the Headmaster at an OU dinner.

Schools need time to settle down after robust reforms. In the early twentieth century Uppingham, like other schools, marked time for too long. It reeled from the double blows of two World Wars, 447 OUs losing their lives in 1914–18, 238 in 1939–45, a shocking total for a school of this size. It was J.C. Royds who, in the words of Bryan Matthews, the school's historian, 'eased us into the modern day'. It was he who introduced academic Tutors to help

LEFT The Sports Centre (*John Wright Photography, Warwick*)
RIGHT Musical ensemble in Thring's Old Schoolroom (*John Wright Photography, Warwick*)

pupils adjust to Sixth Form work. During the turbulent late 1960s he refused to abolish compulsory Chapel, which is still compulsory three days a week, as is the lay assembly on the other three. But he did break the monopoly of the big team games, encouraged minor sports and introduced Community Service as an alternative to the CCF. Not till 1975, a year after he left, was the great step taken of admitting girls, and now after ten years they are an essential part of the scene. Sixty of them are housed in the converted school sanatorium.

The central area of the school, with its small courts or quadrangles, creates a friendly, reassuring atmosphere. There are no wide, intimidating expanses. Boys in black jacket, dark trousers, white shirt and school tie thread their way between the Tower Block and School House, past the spreading lime tree on Chapel Lawn. The girls wear grey skirts with their black jackets. Those lads carrying an umbrella – or wearing a boater in summer – are school Praepostors. The name was imported by Thring from Eton, along with such titles as House Captain and Captain of the School. Uppinghamians abbreviate the former to 'Pollies'. To reach other buildings you go out into High Street. Down the road are the new Sixth Form Centre, the Science Block, whose Biology department was opened by Prince Philip in 1957, and the enormous Sports Centre which has caused such structural problems. The swimming pool adjoining has been there for a hundred years. Thring's Gymnasium, the first in an English Public School, is now the theatre.

The boarding Houses are very varied in style, the Lodge being a Victorian extravaganza, Constables a former workhouse. The Houses – there are twelve boys' Houses plus one girls' – are quintessential to the character of Uppingham. Numbers have been deliberately kept within a limit of fifty, so that the Housemaster really knows all his pupils. Despite its administrative attractions central feeding has not been introduced here. Each House sits down to meals together and on its own. Lunch is presided over by Housemaster, Matron and sometimes the Housemaster's wife. This fosters the strong community spirit and reinforces the independence of Housemasters which Thring regarded as so important. Masters – and visitors too – are invited to lunch round the Houses. No Common Room lunch is provided for staff. The Housemaster liaising with the Form Master supervises a boy's work for the first three years. It is through the Housemaster that the Headmaster works, and though he goes round Houses he would never do so without an invitation. Housemasters delegate a great deal of responsibility to their Pollies. There is no individual fagging; junior boys do communal tasks that benefit the whole House. In spite of the architectural variety of the Houses the system of accommodation is roughly the same. Boys start in a junior dormitory, in a little cubicle enclosed by a partition, and move up to a larger and more enclosed cubicle in a senior dorm. Daytime studies are shared and more senior pupils have their own private studies. Bed-sitters are few and far between. The allocation of studies is done by senior boys in a friendly and humane rather than hierarchical way. 'This is Smith's room. It's a big one for a yearling, but he decorated it himself so we let him keep it. This is James Carleton's. It's a nice place to work late at night and he can be his own boss.'

The Common Entrance standard at 50 per cent is 'accessible'. This school takes care not to be an academic forcing house, so in 1984 the 'fast stream' was abolished. The number of Ordinary Levels taken is usually seven to ten. In the Sixth Form twenty-one subjects are available from four different time-table groups, plus a General Studies programme. In the preference of the pupils Science, with Geology available, has a slight edge over the Arts subjects. In an average year about 20 boys and girls go on to Cambridge or Oxford, 60 to other Universities, 25 to Polytechnics and 24 to other institutions of Higher Education. In 1983/4, eight Uppinghamians won academic Awards to Oxbridge, and three won various choral and music Awards.

The catchment area for Uppinghamians has naturally shrunk. More than ever the majority are from the rural areas of Leicestershire and contiguous counties. This accounts for a more friendly and less materialistic kind of boy than you get with an urban or city catchment. But last year there were 50 from overseas, including 19 from Hong Kong, 5 from the United States and 1 from Sabah (formerly North Borneo). The school mounted an expedition to Sahab in 1984 to carry out ambitious pioneering projects – sub-aqua, rock-climbing, forest surveys and the first canoe descents of white-water rivers. Uppingham has a pioneering tradition. When the Canadian West was being opened up it provided more 'gentleman ranchers' than

LEFT The Tower, the Victoria and West classrooms (*photo A. Wilson*)
RIGHT The Thring Centre, formerly the Manor House (*photo A. Wilson*)

The East classrooms and the oriel window of the School Hall, from the Colonnade
(*photo A. Wilson*)

any other Public School, according to the Old Uppinghamian news sheet.

Since the diversification of games in Royd's time, the dominance of team games has lessened, but the inter-house competitions still generate the old enthusiasm and rivalry. Uppingham fields a very good Cricket XI, capable of winning all its matches in some seasons (the Test cricketer Jonathan Agnew is an OU), and its Rugby XV holds its own against good Rugger schools. Cross-country running is stimulated by the Routh, an annual race of $5\frac{1}{2}$ miles; there is now a Cup for the first girl to finish. The main games for girls are Lacrosse and Tennis, and Hockey is played in the Lent Term. However, the sport in which the school has the most remarkable record is full-bore shooting. The Shooting VIII won the Ashburton Shield four times in the years 1976–82, so it is appropriate that the present Headmaster is a full-bore expert. The CCF strides nobly along its paths to glory with a role of 350 boys, but the alternative of Community Service is an Uppingham strength. It was one of the first in this field and has won the NatWest Project Respond prize five times.

Not richly endowed and with no valuable land to sell off, Uppingham has had to rely on Appeals. Its former pupils are loyal and even when far away may send their sons, or daughters, to their old school; 28 per cent of the present pupils are children of OUs, as high a percentage as Harrow. In 1984 there were four brothers of different ages in West Deyne. The quatercentenary Appeal had reached £450,000 by 1984. These funds have paid for improved classrooms, the Sixth Form Centre, the Science Schools extension, Music Schools and an additional music scholarship and bursary. A fresh Appeal will be launched in 1985.

Oakham School

UPPINGHAM'S SISTER FOUNDATION SIX MILES TO THE NORTH WAS ALSO celebrating its quatercentenary in 1984 as well as celebrating one of the great success stories of recent decades. Until 1970 Oakham was a good local Direct Grant Grammar School of 500 boys. The Headmaster, John Buchanan, saw that the cult for comprehensive schools and the abolition of the Direct Grant would put Oakham out on a limb, so in 1970, with the support of an extra-ordinarily generous benefactor, he led the school into independence. In 1971 he went co-educational, launched three development campaigns and under-took an ambitious building programme. In 1977 he was succeeded by Richard Bull, an Eton housemaster, under whom the growth and develop-ment continued. The sixty-acre site occupies much of the north-eastern part of the town with numerous new buildings spreading out from the original School House near the Market and Church. Now there are 500 boys and 400 girls.

Oakham has provided an example for other schools in several important ways. It had the courage to go independent, and to provide full co-education over the whole age-range, for day pupils as well as boarders. At least seventeen Scholarships (Jerwood Scholarships) are available annually. Entry can now be at any age from 10 to 12 for the Lower School, at 13 for the Middle School or at about 16 for the Upper School. The House system aims to mitigate the size of the school but it is on a 'horizontal' basis, grouping pupils of the same age together. Boys and girls in their last year live in a separate House.

The emphasis is on the development of adult responsibility at an early age rather than on a tight disciplinary system. The school is strong on drama, art, music and all liberal activities. It is a friendly, creative and studious place which will become more and more prominent on the Public School map.

Oakham School. Jerwoods, a complex of four junior houses comprising the Prep department (*Oakham School*)

Uppingham School

ADDRESS Rutland LE15 9QE

FOUNDATION 1584 by Robert Johnson, later Archdeacon of Leicester

GOVERNING BODY The Trustees

TITLE OF HEAD AND NUMBER OF TEACHING STAFF Headmaster + 74 (excluding visiting teachers)

TOTAL NUMBER OF PUPILS 635

NUMBER IN SIXTH FORM 300

NUMBER OF ADVANCED LEVEL CHOICES AVAILABLE 21

NAMES OF FORMS (i) Shell and Fourth (ii) Lower Fifth (iii) Upper Fifth (iv) Lower Sixth (v) Middle Sixth (vi) Upper Sixth

PRINCIPAL GAMES, BY TERMS *Michaelmas* Rugby *Lent* Hockey and Cross-Country *Summer* Cricket, Athletics, Tennis.

NAMES OF HOUSES
Boys Brooklands, Constables, Farleigh, Fircroft, The Hall, Highfield, The Lodge, Lorne House, Meadhurst, School House, West Bank, West Deyne
Girls Fairfield, Johnsons (from 1986)

APPLICATION AND ENTRY Registration any time after birth; application possible for a particular House. Entry for boys at 13+, girls at 15/16+

SCHOLARSHIPS, ETC.
Scholarships at 13+ from 20% to 66% of fees
Exhibitions at 13+ worth at least 10% of fees
At least one Sixth Form Scholarship of up to 66% of fees
2 Music Scholarships at 13+ of up to 50% of fees
1 Sixth Form Music Scholarship of up to 50% of fees
Several Music Exhibitions
A number of closed awards (eg for Clergy, Forces, OUs, etc)

BOOK *By God's Grace* by Bryan Matthews

Oundle School

750 BOARDING BOYS

140 DAY BOYS (in Laxton School)

THE NORTHERN END OF THE COUNTY OF NORTHAMPTONSHIRE WAS once called Oundle. The name is so old that experts have given up trying to discover its derivation. The small market town which now bears that name has few other industries except the Public School which provides its *raison d'être*, in the same way as a coal mine feeds the life of a colliery town.

William Laxton was born in Oundle, about 1500. After leaving the Grammar School there he went to London, made his name as a grocer, rose to be Master of the Worshipful Company of Grocers, Lord Mayor of London and a Knight. In his Will he bequeathed property to the Grocers Company on condition that they supported a school and almshouses at Oundle. He died in 1556. Four hundred and thirty years later the school is still governed by the same Worshipful Company. In 1876 it was divided into two parts – a Classical School for those aspiring to University and a Modern School, mainly for Oundle residents. Today Laxton School is a day school linked to Oundle for classes, but with separate games and assemblies.

Oundle remained obscure until 1892 when R.W. Sanderson was appointed. He was one of the historic Headmasters and during his thirty years in office the number of pupils rose from a handful to 583. He was a pioneer, the next step on from Arnold of Rugby and Thring of Uppingham, and by 1922 he had put Oundle on the map as a major Public School. He had entered Durham University to study Theology but graduated with a first class degree in Maths and Physics, and as an Assistant Master at Dulwich he had transformed the teaching of Science and Engineering. Oundle soon discovered that the new Headmaster was something else again, and the boys found an appropriate nickname for him, 'Beans'. Within eight years all but three of the staff had left. However, numbers were rising, so the parents at least must have approved. By 1900 a total of 250 was envisaged and Sanderson had the full support of the Grocers for his new concept.

His contribution to the Public School was that he saw Science, in its widest sense, as having equal advantages with Classics and literary studies. He believed in diversifying the available options. 'Find out what a boy wants to do and let him do it.' Oundle expanded, sprouted a Chapel, a Great Hall, new classrooms. Additional boarding Houses were built and as houses in the town fell vacant they were bought. Most important of all, though, was Sanderson's pet hobby-horse, the Engineering Side. The marvellous Work-

TOP Gateway tower
(*photo Tim Jackson*)
ABOVE The playing fields
(*photo James McConnell*)
RIGHT Exit from morning assembly
(*photo James Shapiro*)

shops he built were unrivalled for fifty years. 'If scientific principles are not learned at school they will never be learned at all.' Annual tuition fees rose to £30. Oundle had become a Science and Engineering school; yet, of the 120 Open Awards won to Cambridge and Oxford during his time 55 were won by the Classical side, as against 69 by the Science side. Sanderson's contribution was that he broadened the scope of Public School education, offering diversified subjects and activities so that every type of boy could find an interest somewhere. He insisted on all the boys singing heartily in the new Chapel he had built and one of his last enterprises was the first performance of Handel's *Messiah* by a school.

The tragic toll of 1914–18 – so many former colleagues and pupils – undermined his health. On 15 June 1922 he gave a lecture on 'The Duty and Service of Science in the New Era' to the Union of Scientific Workers at University College, London. His great friend H.G. Wells was in the Chair. That speech was his last utterance. He died a few minutes after finishing it.

The Chapel is a War Memorial but in a sense it is also a memorial to Sanderson. His ashes were placed in a niche in the Ambulatory, behind the high altar. They face Hugh Easton's glass windows depicting the seven ages

The Chapel (*photo James McConnell*)

of man. First is the schoolboy 'creeping like snail unwillingly to school', with below it another inscription: 'You who are young – see now your dream – see now your vision'. The three chancel windows above the altar were created by John Piper and Patrick Reyntiens in 1956. The nine lights dramatically depict the nine abstract and eternal qualities of the Son of God; the first six represent the Way, the Life, the Truth, the Vine, the Bread of Heaven, the Water of Baptism and Regeneration, and the last three the Judge, the Teacher, the

Good Shepherd. The Chapel stands clear and apart. You approach it through spacious lawns broken by clumps of birch trees, lilacs, a rock garden in which is a statue of a naked little boy, the gift of Sanderson. The model was Peter Scott and the sculptress was his mother. Scott of the Antarctic's last message had been, 'For God's sake look after our people. . . .' Peter was sent to Oundle, where he acquired his passion for birds.

West of the Chapel on high ground are the playing fields: Rugby pitch, Cricket pitch and a cinder athletics track. (Oundle's Rugby XV has a particularly high reputation.) From here the school spills down into the town, over the A427 which runs through it. The hub is the Cloisters opposite the old School House, which now contains the principal offices. Boys' boarding Houses – there are no girls at Oundle – vary from the ancient in the town to the modern up among the fields, with sixty-five to seventy boys in each. House-masters are assisted by one resident Tutor and several other masters who each supervise the work and general activities of a clutch of boys. Feeding arrangements vary, some Houses having their meals in the House, others going to a refectory where several Houses have a separate dining-room but share a kitchen. Living accommodation varies and tends to be crowded. In general, you spend three or four terms in a 'prep room' and then move to a large study which you share, the number diminishing from five in a study to two. Meanwhile you sleep, possibly in a bunk-bed, in a large open dormitory with no partitions and move on to a smaller partitioned dormitory. In the end you may get a bed-sitter to yourself.

As elsewhere, personal fagging has gone and instead junior boys are allotted tasks to keep the House clean and tidy. Every House runs a Senior bar at set times during the week, to which masters and boys from other Houses may be invited. All these factors emphasize that however much the school has changed the House remains the most important unit in a boy's life. In his autobiography *Life's rich pageant* Arthur Marshall gives a marvellously witty account of his life here as a boy, teacher and Housemaster.

Most Oundelians have no complaint that this has remained purely a boys' school. They comment that when they visit schools with 'co-ed' Sixth Forms the boys seem less natural, more inclined to adopt attitudes to impress the girls. Plenty of time for girls, they say, in the holidays. Perhaps in term-time too, for the rules have been relaxed so that boys can make friends in the town. Relations are good between the townsfolk and the boys in their uniform tweed jackets, grey flannels, white shirt and tie.

For the sixteen years up to 1984 Oundle was again under the Headmaster-ship of a scientist, and by pure chance his Second Master was a scientist also, but this does not signify any special emphasis on Science today, for the preference of Sixth Formers is equally balanced between the Humanities and the Sciences. The school's results in public examinations are eminently

OPPOSITE Harrow. The Old School (*photo David Herbert*)

respectable, with about forty a year going on to Cambridge and Oxford. In the last round of Awards Oundelians won six Scholarships and Exhibitions.

O and A Level statistics show a school's performance in examinations, but they do not reveal a whole other vital area of school life, where some of the most important things about Oundle are happening. Firstly, there are the steps taken to make a small community look outwards. There is, of course, community service locally, but this has extended, for instance, to giving a couple of dozen children from a Catholic area of Belfast a summer holiday over here. Sixth Form historians have visited the European Communities' Institutions, have attended a study week in Berlin and gone through the Wall. Oundle has established a link with a school in Hungary beyond the Iron Curtain, and was the first school in the world allowed to go right across China to scale two 20,000 foot virgin peaks. In a link with Papua New Guinea boys have made contact in the Highlands with inhabitants of Stone Age villages and are now raising £3,000 to irrigate their valley. A Peace Group was given leave to travel up to London and attend a CND rally in Hyde Park, and speakers visiting the school have included such controversial figures as Jack Jones, Ken Livingstone and Red Robbo. The new Stahl Theatre in West Street was named after Rodolphe Stahl, who was only at Oundle 1900–02 but believed he owed his success to those two years and subsequently gave the school a handsome benefaction. The theatre was once a church, so you walk under a covered way past buttresses to enter a modern auditorium with seating for 250. Fourteen plays a year are produced, seven of them House plays, and with its visiting groups, ballet and opera the theatre has become a cultural centre for the area.

Oundle is exceptional in keeping its very full prospectus up to date annually. From it we learn that 40 per cent of the pupils in 1984 came from East Anglia and the eastern Midlands and 10 per cent from overseas, while 28 per cent were the sons of OOs, a number on a par with Harrow or Uppingham. Many of today's parents represent a type new to the Public School, people who have made their own way in the world and are aware of what a modern education must provide, what qualities the modern school-leaver must possess. Britain has been reluctant to become a technological nation and our schools have perhaps been slow to wake up to the needs of the age we live in. Sanderson's Workshops (which are still in daily use) with their lathes, oxy-acetylene gas, electric arc welders, 5-ton capacity crane, multi-media design area and traditional wood-shop reflected a society that had been forced to industrialize willy-nilly. The new Microelectronics Centre, also named the Lyon Centre, is a step in a new and tangential direction. The first such centre

OPPOSITE ABOVE Christ's Hospital. The Grecians' Arch, Lamb House and the Avenue from the top of Chapel tower (*photo Neil Fleming*)

OPPOSITE BELOW Charterhouse. After Sunday Chapel, with the statue of Thomas Sutton in the background (*photo Roger Smeeton*)

Chemistry lesson (*photo James Shapiro*)

in any school, it was opened by Sir Keith Joseph on 16 February 1983. It has three classrooms – a computer room, a computer systems room and an electronics room. All boys, at every level of the school, are taken out of main stream subjects to come here for one block week of total immersion every year. For first- and second-year boys the emphasis is on familiarization, the third year learns BASIC, the fourth year Electronics. In the fifth year boys combine computing with electronics, and the work develops *ad hoc* as new frontiers are explored; one group might be inter-facing computers, another working on robotics, another on word processing. An advanced group will do systems software development, printed circuit-board manufacture, data base management systems and activities on the fringe of the possible. There is constant liaison with outside industry through a local area network. A spin off has been OSFAX, Oundle School's own internal information service, completely designed and built here on the lines of CEEFAX.

Thus every boy leaving the school should be fully equipped to meet the challenge of the technological revolution, or indeed anybody else's Revolution.

Oundle School

ADDRESS Oundle, Peterborough PE8 4EN

FOUNDATION 1556 by William Laxton

GOVERNING BODY Master, Warden and Court of Assistants of the Worshipful Company of Grocers

TITLE OF HEAD AND NUMBER OF TEACHING STAFF Headmaster + 81 (excluding visiting teachers)

TOTAL NUMBER OF PUPILS 890

NUMBER IN SIXTH FORM 300

NUMBER OF ADVANCED LEVEL CHOICES AVAILABLE 15

NAMES OF FORMS (i) Third (ii) Fourth (iii) Fifth (iv) Lower Sixth (v) Upper Sixth

PRINCIPAL GAMES, BY TERMS *Michaelmas* Rugby *Lent* Hockey, Athletics *Summer* Cricket, Rowing

NAMES OF HOUSES
Boarding School, Grafton, Bramston, Dryden, Crosby, St Anthony, New, Laxton, Sanderson, Sidney, Laundimer, The Berrystead (age 11–13)
Day Laxton School

APPLICATION AND ENTRY Registration any time up to entry at 11+ or 13+

SCHOLARSHIPS, ETC.
1 Grocer's Company Scholarship of £3,780 p.a.
12 Scholarships of from £900 to £2,836 p.a.
1 Scholarship of £500
4 Continuation Scholarships for boys 11+, £567 for 2 years at preparatory school and £1,134 for 5 years at Oundle
2 Junior Awards for boys 11+, entering the Junior House

BOOK *A History of the Oundle Schools* by W.G. Walker

Harrow School

HARROW IS ALMOST AS WORLD-FAMOUS AS ETON. THE NAMES OF THE two schools were publicized by the annual Eton and Harrow Match at Lord's cricket ground, which in Victorian times became a main event in the London season so that by 1910 as many as 15,000 spectators were present. Champagne corks popped on the coaches of the nobility and gentry parked three deep round the ground. The Lord's match is now a mere one-day affair, and its decline reflects a profound change in Public School attitudes.

Harrow stands on 'the Hill' ten miles from the City of London, on whose summit in 1094 Saint Anselm consecrated the Church of St Mary. The church with its ancient yew trees is an oasis of quiet surrounded by a village and a school whose buildings cascade down the slopes to the flat lands below. Approaching Harrow today you drive through a sprawling suburbia, climb a steep hill which brings you through the village and then suddenly the sight of a flurry of boys wearing straw hats tells you that you are in a school.

There is no central quadrangle and the hub of the place is the comparatively small space in front of the Old Schools known as Bill Yard, because it was here that the Head Master used to 'take Bill', the daily roll-call. The Old Schools, in which the original Fourth Form Room with its birching block and hundreds of carved names is still preserved, dates from 1571, the year in which William Lyon founded the school. He was the largest landowner in the neighbourhood and his estate included a piece of ground in London called Shepherd Market. In his Will he provided for a grammar school to give free education to thirty local boys, and stipulated that the governors 'shall not receive any girl into the school'. It was not until two hundred years later, under the Headmastership of Dr Joseph Drury, that it really flourished and grew. By the time he retired in 1805 this great Head Master had raised the number of boys to 345 and had turned out four Prime Ministers – Lord Goderich, Sir Robert Peel, Lord Aberdeen and Spencer Perceval. It was now established as a rival to Eton and many of the leading families preferred it, but it underwent a bad patch up to 1845 when discipline collapsed. The boys became the scandal of the district and numbers fell to sixty-nine. When he was appointed Head Master, C.J. Vaughan, who had served under Arnold at Rugby, saw organized games as a counter-attraction to bullying, poaching and stone-throwing, approved the formation of the famous Philathletic Club and established a monitorial system intended primarily to organize games. Thus began the much-derided cult of athleticism in the Public Schools, with the star performers, or 'bloods', acquiring greater prestige than the scholars. Numbers rose to nearly 500 and by the First World War Harrow had sent forth two more lads who were destined to become Prime Ministers, Stanley Baldwin and Winston Churchill. It was favoured by eminent foreigners; two other great leaders were educated there, Pandit Nehru and King Hussein.

Churchill has recorded how at Harrow he failed in Latin and as a consequence learned the structure of the English sentence from Mr Somerville. It could be argued that this obscure schoolmaster contributed to the salvation of the free world. In the Library, designed by Gilbert Scott, there is a section devoted to the works of W.S. Churchill. A bibliography tells us that 200 books have been written about him, his own published works number 140, not counting 525 articles for papers and periodicals.

Largely because application for entry is made to a Housemaster and not the Head Master, the importance and individuality of the House at Harrow is particularly marked. The Houses themselves are mostly former private residences standing in their own grounds; Grove, for instance, once belonged to R.B. Sheridan. Numbers in a House may be as high as ninety, which makes it more difficult than at, say, Uppingham, for a Housemaster to make the rounds of the rooms in the evening, though he has the assistance of one resident and two non-resident Tutors. More responsibility therefore falls on the Monitors, whose disciplinary sanctions may include 'jerks' – stringent

Harrow School Room. Aquatint by Havell after Pugin, from Ackermann's *Public Schools* 1816 (*British Museum*)

tasks of the physical or mental variety. You have to be quite a tough character to enjoy life here. In some Houses there is still fagging, which usually means doing communal tasks. Where personal fagging survives it is by mutual agreement between a Monitor and a junior boy, with appropriate remuneration for the fag. Accommodation varies according to the House, but usually after two or three terms of sharing a boy has a bedroom–study to himself.

The Houses mingle with classrooms and other buildings and do not obstruct the skyline because of the fall of the hill. To a Harrovian 'the Hill', which he shares with the local village community, evokes the whole ethos of his school. The area beyond which he may not go without permission is bounded by the bottom of the Hill, and the words 'banned from the Hill' have a Dantesque finality. From this high viewpoint the surrounding urban sprawl is softened by trees and green slopes, while at night the distant lights of London sparkle as temptingly as diamonds.

As elsewhere, the majority of parents now live within a hundred miles and the percentage of OHs, 28 per cent, is falling, but many still come from distant parts of the British Isles with a considerable number from abroad. If the catchment is shrinking in the geographical sense it is broadening in social terms and the spread of academic ability is also wide. The number of day boys has shrunk to 'one or two', though 470 day boys are provided for at the John Lyon School down the hill. No girls are admitted to the school, bar a couple of masters' daughters. A traditional link with the USA is kept alive by the Harrow School Association over there and a regular flow of graduates from American secondary schools comes to take the Sixth Form Courses on the Hill. Though the majority of boys attend the services in the Gilbert Scott Chapel – two per week plus one on Sundays – 16 other religions are represented here, the 70 Roman Catholics and the 60 Jews having their own rooms for worship.

The picture of Harrow in the mid-1980s is of innovation against a background of tradition. During the post-war period and the uneasy 1960s Harrow changed little, while other schools undertook programmes of building and reconstruction, or abandoned practices that had become outmoded. This has proved to be an advantage, because the preservation of the more obvious traditions enables much more subtle changes to be made. 'Bill', the daily roll-call in front of the Old Schools, used to be a formal ceremony when every boy answered his name, passing in front of the Head Master with the school *Custos*, a sort of beadle, and the Monitors standing by. (The Queen 'took Bill' on her visit in 1971.) Since 1978 Bill has only been taken on special occasions, but Harrovians still wear a uniform of blue jacket, grey flannels, white shirt and black tie, plus a straw hat. The straw hat, a problem on windy days, adds a distinctive touch to the inevitable unkemptness of schoolboys. A Blood wears the school crest on his 'straw', a Triple Blood with three crests is the cynosure of envying eyes. Tails are worn on Sundays and formal occasions with perhaps a top hat and umbrella, School Monitors on appointment still receive a key from the Head Master as a token of trust and hand it back when

St. Mary's Church, Harrow on
the Hill (*photo David Herbert*)

'Bill' on Speech Day
(*Harrow Photo Club*)

they leave, masters wear suits and gowns for teaching and when in the
Masters' Room, and every summer one of Shakespeare's plays is produced in
a replica of the Globe Theatre and in the tradition of the Elizabethan stage.
Above all, 'Songs' continue – Songs in Houses, Songs when the whole school
gathers in the Assembly Hall. Songs are a unifying experience shared by all
Harrovians, even when they meet many years afterwards. In the darkest days
of the War, Churchill used to come down here to be uplifted by songs such as
'Forty Years On'.

The many changes which have occurred under a new headmagisterial regime
are more significant than uniforms, or the parochial terminology of a school.
The academic standard has been pulled up by its bootstraps, with more
emphasis at the bottom of the school on Science and less on Latin, which is
no longer required for University entrance. Classrooms have been improved,
with masters teaching on carpets rather than bare boards, the Head Master
has placed himself more at the centre of things and brought his staff and
Monitors more into the decision-making process. Change usually costs money
and Harrow has property rather than endowments in the shape of the 600-
acre Northchurch estate, Shepherd Market having been sold off long ago.
So in 1976 an on-going Appeal was launched and this has helped to fund an
extensive programme of building and improvement. The Old Speech Room
Gallery has been converted into a Museum housing the collection of paintings
and Egyptology, an Industrial and University Centre (the Butler Centre) has
been opened, a Sixth Form Club with spacious rooms and bars provides a
meeting-place for senior boys as well as masters and parents. The Modern
Language Department has been given a complete face-lift and a new Maths–
Physics block and Resources Centre is already in use, the latter available to
all masters. Not before time the boarding Houses are being refurbished, the
renewing of The Knoll enabling boys to be decanted into the spare House
while the work is done.

Another change of emphasis is the creation of a new Club, the Guild,
which is intended to give prestige to cultural and intellectual distinction and
offset the dominance of the Philathletic Club. Its members wear a special tie
and are expected to join Monitors and the Phil in carrying out official duties.
But the feature which has made most difference is the Churchill Shepherd
Hall. Formerly the boys used to have all their meals in their own Houses,
now the whole school gathers in this huge dining hall. The slope of the hill
makes the building, like many of its neighbours, inconspicuous. From above
it is not unlike a long bungalow but in fact it has three storeys, and its
windows command pleasing views. Lunch is taken by Houses, but for other
meals boys sit where they like. This has broken down the insularity of Houses
and encourages Harrovians to make friends throughout the school. There is
now less cliquishness between members of different Houses, the old hierarchical age-group barriers have broken and the use of Christian names is
more general. All this has made the Head Master a more central, visible and
approachable dignitary, vying with the Housemaster as the most crucial

The school farm (*Harrow Photo Club*)

'beak' in a boy's life. The Head Master takes lunch at a table in the centre where all can see him, with his Monitors and any visitors to the school. At the end of lunch the Head of School makes his announcements through a public address system. Masters lunch together here and may sign in for dinner. This has brought more cohesion to a very large staff and enhanced the principal emphasis in the school today – communication.

The Head Master now addresses all new parents and sends them a news letter every term. He has a weekly meeting with his Monitors, when the discussion is more likely to be about the well-being of boys than about discipline. Communication in the technical sense has been achieved by the replacement of the old telephone system. Harrow, with its 200 telephones, now has a bigger system, a Monarch, than any village in the UK and the whole place has been linked by computers. The Bursary's records are computerized, any master can use the facilities in the Resources Centre and by using the terminal beside his desk the Head Master can instantly call up information about any boy in the school. It goes without saying that Computer Studies are started in the first year, and that computers are available to all boys.

This communication has also been extended outwards. Boys go down the hill not only to play games on the comparatively flat playing fields below or to bathe in Duckers, the largest swimming pool in Britain. Within the estate is a farm, run by the boys, whose dairy herd produces seventy gallons of milk a day. That's enough to supply the whole school, delivery being made by

boys before breakfast, with some left over for the Milk Marketing Board.
Not content with that, they've started breeding calves and pigs as well. The
Harrow Club in London, developed from the old Harrow Mission, is in
Notting Dale near the Westway. Known locally as 'Harrow', it is a broadly-
based community centre. Its steel band is a swinging feature of the Notting
Hill Carnival. Here also is the seat of the country's first Urban Studies
Centre, which merits a whole article to itself.

Duckers being an open-air pool is expensive to maintain and heat, so
architect's plans have been completed for a new swimming pool and sports
hall which is to be an amenity for local people as well as the school. Already
the 9-hole golf course, opened in 1978, is available to local players, and
Stanmore Rifle Club shares the shooting facilities.

On the whole the teaching at Harrow is good, and the relationship between
boys and 'beaks' has become more friendly. The curriculum is based on 36
periods a week.

1ST YEAR (SHELLS) Divinity, English, History, Geography, Science, Latin,
Mathematics including Computer Studies, French. Plus Art, Handicraft,
Workshops and PE

2ND YEAR (REMOVES) *Options* Greek and German instead of History and
Geography. Classical Studies instead of Latin
O Level Religious Studies

3RD YEAR (FIFTH FORM) O LEVEL YEAR All take English Language and
Literature, Maths, French, a Science; plus a combination of: History, Geography, Biology, Physics, Chemistry, Greek, German or Latin.
4 O Level passes are required for promotion to the Sixth Form

4TH AND 5TH YEARS (LOWER AND UPPER SIXTH) Normally three subjects
are taken to Advanced Level, each having seven or eight time-tabled periods.
One subject is chosen from Group A, B and C. Group D are additional
options.

Group A	Group B	Group C	Group D
Art	Art	Art	Ancient History*
Biology	Classical Civilization	Chemistry	Geology
Economics		Design (Technology)	Music
English	English		History of Art
French	Geography	Economics	Mathematics
Mathematics	Latin with Roman History	German	Religious Studies*
	Latin	Greek	
	Physics	History	*1-year course

Non-specialist subjects are regarded as equally important. Three subjects, each having three or four periods per week, are chosen from the eighteen available: CDT (Craft, Design, Technology), Art, German, Italian, Russian, Spanish, French with Business Studies, Mathematics/Physics, Music, General Studies, English, Computer Studies, Economic and Social History, Facts of Economic Life, Latin, Greek.

For the first three years work is overseen by the form master, who reports to the Housemaster. Harrow takes a great deal of trouble to see that in his last term before entering the Sixth Form a boy – and his parents – are fully briefed. A 24-page booklet, *Sixth Form Choices*, sets out all the options. It emphasizes that 'industry has just as much to offer as many of the so-called professions', and that 'career patterns of the past do not necessarily reflect the needs and aspirations of the present'. During his year in the Lower Sixth Form each boy has a work Tutor, one of the masters teaching him, to guide him in this period of transition. He also receives an excellent booklet *How to Study*, by a Harrow School beak, which is a pearl of wisdom.

Monitors and Juniors in formal Sunday dress
(*Harrow Photo Club, A. Grant*)

The Head Master was not willing to divulge Ordinary and Advanced Level results to the author of a book – and that is a privilege of independent schools which do not participate in the Assisted Places scheme – but he claimed that in a recent year Harrow was in the top eight boarding schools gaining Awards at Cambridge and Oxford. In the last 'league table' of such results (*Times Educational Supplement*, 27 April 1984) nine awards were won by Harrovians.

One of Harrow's most impressive buildings is the War Memorial. It commemorates 650 Harrovians killed in 1914–18, when eight VCs were won. The panelling in the Alex Finch room upstairs is from Brook House, where Queen Elizabeth I held her first court, and the floorboards are from the deck of HMS *St Vincent*. A lamp burns perpetually over the portrait of Alex Finch, killed in September 1918. On the ground floor the busts of Churchill and Alexander remind us that nearly 400 more were killed in 1939–45.

Harrow School

ADDRESS Harrow-on-the-Hill, Middlesex HA1 3HW

FOUNDATION 1571 by John Lyon

TITLE OF HEAD AND NUMBER OF TEACHING STAFF Head Master + 76 (excluding visiting teachers)

TOTAL NUMBER OF PUPILS 750

NUMBER IN SIXTH FORM 348

NUMBER OF ADVANCED LEVEL CHOICES AVAILABLE 23

NAMES OF FORMS (i) Shell (ii) Remove (iii) Fifth (iv) Lower Sixth (v) Upper Sixth

PRINCIPAL GAMES, BY TERMS *Autumn* Rugby *Lent* Harrow football, soccer *Summer* Cricket

NAMES OF HOUSES
Newlands, Moretons, The Grove, Rendalls, The Park, The Knoll, Druries, West Acre, Bradbys, Elmfield, The Head Master's

APPLICATION AND ENTRY Application via a Housemaster. Entry at 12–13

SCHOLARSHIPS, ETC.
12 Scholarships and Exhibitions, from £100 p.a. to 100% fees
4 Music Scholarships, from £150 to 100% fees
1 Art Scholarship, from £150 to 50% fees

BOOK *Harrow School Yesterday and Today* by E.D. Laborde

Christ's Hospital

IF HARROW HAS JUST ABOUT THE HIGHEST FEES OF ANY SCHOOL IN THIS book, Christ's Hospital, near Horsham in Sussex, has the lowest. The older Public Schools were founded to provide education for the poor. In most of them 'the poor' survive only as a small nucleus of Scholars admitted through a very demanding examination. At Christ's Hospital the needy form the main body of the school. To qualify, parents of a one-child family must have an income below £9,000 p.a. and some pupils pay no fees at all, even receive an allowance for pocket money. Only one quarter of the school's running costs comes from fees, which means that the average parent pays a quarter of what the full fees would be – currently about £3,750. The rest comes from Donation Governors' contributions and endowments which have accrued over the years. None of it comes from the State or the local authority, and yet, as we shall see, the provisions for education of a high standard are excellent.

In another significant way this 'Blue-Coat School' is different. All pupils enter between the age of 10.3 and 12, two years earlier than at most Public Schools. The word pupils is used because there has until now been a sister school for girls in Hertford with a roll of 300. The finances of both are administered by the Clerk of Christ's Hospital in Great Tower Street, London, and by the time this book is published the two schools will have become one.

The entry system is complicated enough to fill a 14-page booklet. The first qualification is need. Broadly-speaking entry is by 'presentation' or by success in 'competitions', i.e. the school's own examination. Nine City of London livery companies and about 300 Donation Governors have the privilege of presenting a candidate, and presentations are also available to the children of persons distinguished in Literature, Art, Science, or who are in the Service of the Crown or who have rendered services to the public or to Christ's Hospital. There are places for London children, and a number of places available under special trusts. All these admissions are dealt with by the Clerk of Christ's Hospital.

The catchment area is now less predominantly London and increasingly Surrey and the neighbouring area. The I L E A discourages the creaming off of able pupils from their comprehensive schools and only sends boys when there is boarding need. Boys come from a wide variety of backgrounds, some of them from very tough areas of London. Many of them have a maturity,

worldly wisdom and awareness of the harsh realities of life that is not found
in other Public Schools. Christ's Hospital has a strong sense of community
and a marked *esprit de corps*, but in many other ways it is quite different from
most schools.

In 1552 the plight of the sick and poor in London was pitiable. The boy
King, Edward VI, was moved by compassion to found three Hospitals:
Bridewell for 'idell vagabondes', St Thomas's for the 'sore and sick' and
Christ's Hospital for the education of children. The school spent its first 350
years in the former Greyfriars Monastery in London. Though a Protestant
foundation it survived Bloody Mary's repression. In the Great Plague of
1665, thirty-two of the 260 pupils perished and in the Great Fire the following year half the buildings were destroyed. Wren and Hawksmoor were
among the architects who planned the rebuilding. In 1673, thanks to the
efforts of Samuel Pepys, a Royal Mathematical School was founded within
the same walls, and Charles II granted a second Royal Charter. During the
next two centuries the Blue Coat boys became a familiar sight in London,
sometimes mistaken for monks in their ankle-length, dark blue habit. Samuel

Aerial view (*photo Neil Fleming*)

LEFT The Cloisters (*photo James McConnell*)
RIGHT Gilt statue of Edward VI in a niche at the end of Big School (*photo Neil Fleming*)

Taylor Coleridge and Charles Lamb wore the 'Housey' coat, and probably the great English Saint, Edmund Campion. In 1864 Christ's Hospital was the first endowed school to be investigated by the Public Schools Commission. It was as a consequence of this that the school moved out of London into the country.

A site of 1,200 acres had been purchased just south of Horsham for £47,500. The buildings were planned by the architects Sir Aston Webb and Ingress Bell and built at a cost of £546,000. Boys and teachers moved down on 27 May 1902 to occupy the buildings which we see today. What they found was a crescent of eight pairs of boarding houses. At the symmetrical centre the Dining Hall formed the north side of a great quadrangle, opposite was Big School, and the Chapel on the east side faced the Science Block on the west. In the centre was a lead statue of Edward VI, brought from the London site, and there are now two other links with the past, the Grecian Arch and the Wren Arch. The premises were a ready-made unit for 820 boys boarding, and so they were to remain for eighty-three years. If the row of

The Hall of Christ's Hospital, London. Aquatint by Stadler after Pugin, from Ackermann's
Public Schools 1816 (*British Museum*)

boarding Houses has a starkly uniform and institutional appearance, the quadrangle is an inspiring space with its tones of mellow brick and Bath stone.
The Chapel's soaring brick columns evoke the English Perpendicular style,
while inside, the murals of Frank Brangwyn wryly echo the fifteenth-century
wall paintings in the Chapel at Eton. The huge Dining Hall can seat the
whole school under the second largest unsupported ceiling in England. One
of the biggest paintings in the world, by Verrio, adorns the north wall; it
depicts girls in the school uniform of 1684, and is a presage of things to come.
The portraits of Victoria and Albert are unique, for both are on horseback,
and the three ceilings of Big School, Chapel and the Dining Hall are architectural masterpieces in their own right.

Among other provisions of the 1902 plan were two big blocks of classrooms, a fine library, a lofty, spacious and well-lit art school, a music school
and a manual school. This last is now a Craft and Design Centre, but still
with six forges. Lavish though the 1902 facilities were, the needs of modern
education have necessitated additions. In 1931 a large new Science Block was
built on one side of the Garden Quad, a name transplanted from London,
and in 1932 a new Music School and Library were added. In 1969 an Appeal
was launched to meet three urgent requirements, the first of which was for
classrooms – in the 1950s the curriculum had expanded; more boys were

staying on to take the new GCE exam at Advanced Level, with the object of
gaining entry to University. The second requirement was more accommodation for music: since the formation of a band in 1868 music had become an
increasingly strong element in the school's life and now half the boys were
learning a musical instrument. Thirdly, it was time to build a theatre.

The new Arts Centre, the latest of these requirements to be met, was
opened in 1970. Designed by the architect Bill Howell, it consists of nine new
classrooms with views over the playing fields, an octagonal concert room for
band practice, extensive music teaching accommodation, an inter-depart-

The Band in front of Dining Hall (*photo Neil Fleming*)

mental library and a theatre. The theatre claims to be the most flexible in the country, its galleried circle and movable towers allowing, for instance, a recreation of the old Globe Theatre. The Centre serves the needs of the district as well as the school and hosts performances by celebrities, though the acoustics make instrumental performance difficult.

The most recent developments have been within existing buildings. Space has been found in the corridors or cloisters for computer and audio-visual rooms, school offices, careers rooms. Even the roof space of the old library is being floored in and put to use.

What has changed very little up till now is the living accommodation for the boys – spartan even by Public School standards. The sixteen Houses stand in pairs which seen from outside appear to be mirror images of each other. Boys stay in a Junior House until they are 13 or 14, then move to a Senior House. Each House has on the ground floor a day-room for twenty-five to thirty boys; first year boys sit at a long central table with benches, while round the walls are sixteen 'toyces', tiered desk-tops that can swing out to form individual work alcoves or be folded back when the whole room is needed. The old changing-rooms at the back have been converted into shared studies for about twenty-five. Most boys sleep in the dormitories on the first and second storeys with their gleaming parquet floors. There are twenty-five in each, of mixed ages, the most junior at one end, the most senior at the other. Best Housey coats are kept in a coat room and ablutions, etc., are in the 'lav-ends'. Some senior boys now have study–bedrooms. Accommodation for the Housemaster and Matron is in the centre of the block or at the back. Each Housemaster has an Assistant Housemaster/ Tutor. One Housemaster and five assistants are women.

Six of the teaching staff are women, one of them a deaconess. They teach a 38-period week, half-holidays being Wednesday and Saturday. Pupils are thus exposed to seven years of teaching by a Public School staff, with up to five years of preparation for Ordinary Levels. The names of the blocks are:

		Average age
1st year	Second Form	11.4
2nd year	Third Form	12.4
3rd year	Little Erasmus (Options)	13.4
4th year	Upper Fourth (some O Levels)	14.4
5th year	Great Erasmus (most O Levels)	15.6
6th year	Deputy Grecians ⎱ Sixth Form (A Levels)	16.5
7th year	Grecians ⎰	17.7

The first two years are on a broad curriculum which includes a course of Computer Studies. On entering Little Erasmus boys choose two subjects out of about fifteen, which they study to O Level. The aim at this stage is to keep open as many academic and career areas as possible. 'He should choose subjects in which he has shown ability and which he enjoys' is the sound advice given. Some O Levels are taken at the end of the fourth year, most at

The Arts Centre (*photo Neil Fleming*)

the end of the fifth. To be admitted to the Sixth Form a pupil must gain five good O Level passes — five Grade Cs are not good enough. His aptitudes and career ambitions are also considered, but those who fail to make the grade have to leave Christ's Hospital. The younger ones may take the Great Erasmus year again, the others leave at once. About forty leave before taking A Level, some going to local schools, some to A Level courses elsewhere, a few into jobs. A careers master, of which there are six, commented that it is easier to find a job at 16 than at 18.

The choice of subjects available to a Deputy Grecian is remarkably wide. Three main subjects are chosen from the available twenty-six, plus two minority subjects out of twenty-one. In Physics, Chemistry and Biology the Nuffield courses are followed. It was a Christ's Hospital master called Armstrong who pioneered the heuristic method of education-by-discovery and the Nuffield scheme continues that concept. Christ's Hospital was founded in the age of Erasmus. It is thoroughly compatible with the spirit of the New Learning that the primacy of Classics does not prevent a strong tradition of Science. In 1984, out of 216 Deputy Grecians and Grecians, 83 were doing A Level Science and Maths and 10 doing Classics. It is very compartmentalized; here they do not combine the Humanities with Science. The next most popular subject after Science is Modern History, in which the special subject might be 'Literature, Learning and the Arts in England, 1485–1625', with appropriate visits to London museums and local houses. The Modern Languages department has native speakers in French, German and Russian, and many lessons are conducted in the language studied. That this pays off in written exams is proved by the 1984 A Level results for French, German and Russian: of 41 candidates, 23 got Grade A (16 with a pass in the S paper), 12 got Grade B, 3 Grade C and 3 Grade D. There were no failures. Many non-Scientists combine Greek, Latin, History, Engineering, Music or Art with English, in which literary analysis and expression is developed and creative writing encouraged. Christ's Hospital boys show unusual depth and maturity in their English essays. A dozen boys have the good sense to choose Design, in which they can earn 60 per cent of their marks for work done throughout the two years.

Comment on achievement in competitions would not be complete without mention of the Duke of Edinburgh's Awards won by Housey boys in 1983/4: 11 Golds and 18 Silvers.

Of the traditions which have been preserved the uniform – black breeches and yellow stockings under a full-length dark-blue coat – is the most striking. Its very eccentricity makes it acceptable and most boys would not want it changed. They go all over the place in their uniform and it is amusing to note the respectful silence which falls on a railway carriage when a Blue-Coat boy steps in. Years of managing the skirted garment gives the senior boys a gait of noticeable and measured dignity which even an Etonian can hardly match. As soon as a boy enters the Sixth Form he becomes a Deputy Grecian and in his last year a Grecian. Those in authority are Button Grecians and wear a metal plaque. The head boy, or Senior Grecian to you, is invested with an aura of immense authority. The most spectacular tradition is the daily ritual for going into the Dining Hall for the midday meal, when the school band comes marching across the great quadrangle, and as the drums and brass echo from the enclosing walls the boys form up by Houses and march in fours into the Hall – speedily and in good order. There, Grace is said from a pulpit brought from Greyfriars in London.

This framework of tradition enables changes of a deeper sort to be made without a loss of balance. Where compulsory Chapel is concerned, the clock has actually been put back a little, for on Mondays, Tuesdays and Wednesdays differing sections of the school are now required to attend the 8.30 a.m. service and on Thursdays the whole school attends. On Sundays a 6.30 p.m. service is voluntary for Sixth Formers but compulsory for boys in the first three years, but all the same a Communion service each Sunday morning attracts about a hundred communicants. It is the attitude to games that has changed more. The dominance of the main team games, Rugger and Cricket, has gone and other games have proliferated, among them hockey, tennis and athletics. No team games are played on Wednesday so as to leave one of the half-holiday afternoons free for such activities as the CCF, for seniors only, or the Scout Troop, which encourages adventure training and ultimately expeditions to the Alps, the Arctic or the Himalayas. Boys in their first three years play no team games on Tuesdays and Thursdays, instead they have a choice of forty different activities. The computerization of these activities allows greater flexibility without tedious administration and supervision.

The careers advisory service, staffed by six masters, has two Careers/ University rooms and every week a double period on careers is set aside for Deputy Grecians. In the first term twenty-one careers are covered – in industry, commerce, the retail trade, the arts, the professions, etc. – with visiting speakers explaining what employers are looking for. In the second term the available choices in Higher Education are covered, and in the third individual interviews are available to boys. Perhaps that is why only two of those who left in 1983 were still seeking employment six months later.

Between the writing of this book and its publication Christ's Hospital will experience the biggest upheaval since it moved out of London. During the nineteenth century the other half of this foundation was growing in reputation and numbers at its home in Hertford. In September 1985 the girls are coming to the Horsham site, creating one co-educational school of about 870. The boys' school has already been run down in numbers to make room for them. There will then be three types of Houses: six senior boys' Houses, six junior boys' Houses and four all-age girls' Houses. Junior girls will occupy the same kind of day-rooms on the ground floor as the boys, with a social room opposite. Seniors will have bed-sitters on the top floor, in the form of small cubicles with thin walls that do not reach the ceiling and curtains instead of doors – by order of the Fire Officer. (In new school buildings every door has to be a fire door.)

Christ's Hospital maintains its links with the City of London, and the band is sometimes invited to march in the Lord Mayor's procession. The Lord Mayor, in full regalia, attends Speech Day at Horsham and every St Matthew's Day about 300 boys go to the Mansion House to receive 'Lord Mayor's largesse'.

Christ's Hospital

ADDRESS Horsham, Sussex RH13 7LS

FOUNDATION 1552 by King Edward VI

GOVERNING BODY Council of Almoners

TITLE OF HEAD AND NUMBER OF TEACHING STAFF Head Master + 83
(excluding visiting teachers)

TOTAL NUMBER OF PUPILS 870 (September 1985; 645 boys, 225 girls)

NUMBER IN SIXTH FORM 250

NUMBER OF ADVANCED LEVEL CHOICES AVAILABLE 26

NAMES OF FORMS (i) Second (ii) Third (iii) Little Erasmus
(iv) Upper Fourth (v) Great Erasmus (vi) Deputy Grecian (vii) Grecian

PRINCIPAL GAMES, BY TERMS *Michaelmas* Rugby *Lent* Soccer, Athletics and Hockey *Summer* Cricket, Tennis, Athletics and Hockey

NAMES OF HOUSES
All divided into A and B: Peele, Thornton, Middleton, Coleridge, Lamb, Barnes, Maine, Leigh Hunt

APPLICATION AND ENTRY By competitive exam or presentation, for entry at age 10.3 on 1 September in year of entry. Entry in September only.

Charterhouse

603 BOARDING BOYS

33 DAY BOYS

78 GIRLS (Sixth Form)

THOMAS SUTTON WAS ONE OF THE WEALTHIEST MEN OF HIS TIME IN England. When he died on 12 December 1611, with his Will under the bedclothes beside him, he had completed the greatest single philanthropic act of the era. In his last months he had seen his desire to found an almshouse and a school confirmed by an Act of Parliament. Charterhouse, in the green fields near Smith Field, had been occupied by Carthusian monks from 1371 until 1535. Then Henry VIII abolished the Monasteries and in one tyrannical stroke swept away a thousand centres of culture and learning. In the course of time Charterhouse passed into the hands of the Earl of Suffolk, from whom Sutton bought it for £13,000.

In this haven of collegiate peace the almshouse and the school thrived for 260 years. One of the schoolmasters, Robert Brooke, refused to accept Cromwell's Solemn League and Covenant and flogged any of his 'Gownboys' who took the oath. He was sacked but not evicted. When his study became a masters' Common Room it was called Brooke Hall and the name is still in use today. Charterhouse survived the Plague by locking its doors and also weathered the Gownboys' Rebellion of 1741. By 1862, however, London had encompassed it. The Public Schools (Clarendon) Commission recommended that it be moved from this morally insalubrious environment. And so Charterhouse acquired a second Founder, the Head Master at that time, Dr Haigh Brown. It was he who located a site in Surrey and persuaded the Governors, amongst whom Royalty has always figured prominently, to build a new school there. When the school part of the dual foundation decamped in 1872, leaving the almshouse in Charterhouse London, one boy in particular was struck by this escape from the urban to the rural scene. His name was R.P. Baden Powell and he was later to found the Scout Movement.

Charterhouse now stands on an airy plateau north of Godalming embraced by the river Wey. It is a place of light and air, of broad vistas and open skies. Its buildings look out over the 200-acre grounds to woodlands, valleys and the more distant Devil's Punchbowl. Their manner is Victorian but of a neo-Gothic upward-thrusting style with tall windows and many spires. The cloisters surrounding Scholars' Court recall the Carthusian monastery.

The eleven boarding Houses bear the names of their 1872 incumbents. Girdlestoneites, however, has always been known to the boys as 'Duckites', because 112 years ago Mr Girdlestone's gait was seen to resemble that of a certain amphibious bird. The difference between the Houses is great. 'Duckites' is a separate establishment on its own. The three In-Houses are in the main Victorian buildings, where they share a kitchen but have their own separate dining-rooms. Boys spend the first three or four terms in a Long Room, where they have a 'carrel', or desk-space, and sleep in a dormitory cubicle. In their second year they get bed-sitters, which are mostly individual. The seven new Houses, across the playing fields half a mile to the west, represent the most extensive boarding-house programme undertaken by any school since 1945. Originally they were on the south-east side of the main block. In the late 1960s the Governors decided that it would be less costly to rebuild than to refurbish. They sold the Houses and the land and used the £2 million to build the new ones. The Head Master, O. Van Oss, had been Lower Master at Eton and had learned a thing or two from the building of new Houses there. The new Houses are identical in plan but set at varied angles. Built of brick they feature a central stairwell with abutting multi-sided spurs. The interiors are uninstitutional and amicable, with short, angled corridors and social areas. Each House has its Long Room and a Private Side for the Housemaster. Most important of all, there is a study-bedroom for every boy. The new Houses share a common eating block where each has its own dining-room served by a central kitchen. The Tower beside it contains flats for masters.

Parents thus have a choice. An old House with its beguiling archaism and its convenient central position? Or a new House with its *confort moderne*, superb views and the regular trudge across the fields to work? Of course, whichever kind of House they're in the boys think it's the best.

House cricket match with new boarding houses in background (*photo Roger Smeeton*)

Other new buildings are the fruits of an Appeal launched in 1976. They are named after Old Carthusians. The John Derry (first man to break the sound barrier) Design and Technology Centre is on an open plan with one wall completely of glass. Extremely well-equipped it is available seven days a week for Carthusians who want to work in wood, concrete, fibreglass, plastic. All 'Yearlings' (first-year boys) have one 'hash' (school period) per week there. Design and Technology is now taken at Ordinary and Advanced Level. In O Level the pass rate for the first three years, 1982–4, was 100 per cent. Of 27 candidates in 1984, 17 got Grade A, 9 Grade B and 1 Grade C, whilst two Advanced Level candidates scored Grades A and B respectively. The Design and Technology exams entail the submission of a portfolio and thus bring in that element so signally lacking in English public examinations – continuous assessment, or 'course work'.

Ben Travers himself laid the foundation stone of the new Theatre. He died before it was opened in 1983 with a performance of his play, *Thark*. The Ben Travers Theatre is sunk in a hollow and has a sloping slate roof that masks its modern interior, which is an uncompromisingly functional cube with retracting seats, cat-walks, computer-controlled lighting and the option to perform plays either in the round or with a thrust stage or through a proscenium arch.

The Ralph Vaughan Williams Music Centre, completed in 1984, includes a rehearsal room for full orchestra as well as rooms for teaching the 350 Carthusians who learn a musical instrument. Amongst the many groups there are two choirs and two symphony orchestras. Three Music scholarships are awarded to new boys every year and Charterhouse keeps a Composer-in-Residence to encourage budding composers. In the years 1981–4 eight Music Awards were won at Cambridge and Oxford Colleges. OCs are prominent in English musical circles, ranging from Planning Manager of the Royal Festival Hall to the pop group *Genesis*.

'Studio' dates from 1968. It provides a seven-days-a-week service for painters, potters and photographers. The presence of girls doing Advanced Level Art has raised the standard, and the inter-House competition, when exhibited on the walls, shows the range and quantity of work done. The Museum has been rehoused next to the Library. Among a wide range of exhibits it contains a cannon from the Armada, the lock from Shakespeare's bedroom door and a display of palaeolithic, neolithic and romano-British artefacts unearthed when the new Houses were being built.

The next big project will be the refurbishment of the Science Block. £1.5 million will be spent in a six-phase scheme. The Science buildings are old-fashioned, though equipment is lavish enough for forty-nine pupils to do their Nuffield Project experiments without any need to share. The swing towards Science is shown by the figures: in 1968 thirty Physics students were being taught by three masters, in 1984 sixty were being taught by five masters. The same trend is seen in Chemistry and Geology, and now Electronics is being introduced at Ordinary Level and Advanced Level.

The teaching staff are known individually as 'beaks' and collectively as 'Brooke Hall'. This is also the name of the building where beaks meet daily for morning coffee and may dine together twice a week. Carthusians speak well of their beaks, for whom the retiring age is 60, and find them very ready to give extra help when needed. The relationship between Brooke Hall and pupils is relaxed and informal. The necessary formality and pressure is provided by a ceremony known as 'Calling Over', when each form master in the Lower School presents his form to the Head Master, either 'in Hall' or 'under Oak', and reports on individual performance. In the Sixth Form this is replaced by 'Predictions', when beaks meet to forecast Advanced Level results on the basis of current performance.

In an average year Advanced Level is taken in 19 subjects. As befits a school which produced Crashaw, Lovelace, Addison and Thackeray (who had ambitions to become Head Master), and whose present staff have written a remarkable number of books, articles and papers, the most popular subject for Advanced Level candidates is English Literature. Last year 85 per cent of English candidates achieved Grade C or better. The Classical tradition was kept alive by 8 who took Latin and 4 who took Greek. About 150 pupils left in 1984; of these 12 won Awards and 18 more got places at Cambridge or Oxford; 50 more went to other Universities and 14 to Polytechnics. Experience suggests that at University half the Carthusians flower and do brilliantly.

A great change in the school was wrought by the arrival of girls in 1974. They are admitted to the Sixth Form and there is now great competition for the sixty places available. The girls 'go home' every night, or rather to lodgings in houses nearby, when the clock strikes ten. They used to be escorted by *two* boys, for safety, but. . . . Well, now a bus takes them to and from their digs, which are sometimes a bit bleak. Daytime is the best part. They are divided up among boys' Houses where they have a share of a study. Really, they need a girls' Common Room somewhere, because they can be subject to critical masculine comment, especially when they first arrive. They participate in the life of the House and school but play their own games – in the athletic sense. Rules for behaviour are implied rather than formal. The relationship between the sexes is generally relaxed and low-key. Common sense advises against deep emotional commitment, and only once has a couple had to leave the school.

The presence of girls has helped to create a more humane atmosphere. The arrogance of the athletic 'bloods' was broken many years ago, fagging and beating by boys vanished in the last decade. Movement from House to House is much freer and, as elsewhere, the divisions between age-groups are less rigid. The more rigorous traditions have been dropped, though much of the Carthusian terminology survives. In addition to 'Brooke Hall' and 'hash', we hear 'banco' (prep), 'ticks' (teams), 'yearlings' (first year), 'postee' (either 'after you' or indicating some kind of privilege). Terms are known as Quarters: Oration Quarter, Long Quarter (the shortest) and Cricket Quarter. Initials

are widely used for beaks, quarters and Houses. Each House celebrates Founder's Day with a feast in its decorated dining-room. At the special Scholars' Feast a 'loving cup' is passed around with due ceremony. During the whole last week of CQ Carthusians go to Chapel all the way round Undergreen, the large cricket field.

Dress is informal – jacket and flannels – but informality has its limits. There are Bounds, though Carthusians may go beyond them with their Housemaster's permission. Bad behaviour is dealt with by a system of escalating sanctions – extra school or detention, lines, rustication, expulsion. And every day there is compulsory Chapel for all, held in the lofty building designed by Sir Giles Scott as the Charterhouse Memorial to those killed in World War I. Carthusians conform in silence but without protest and a majority of boys appear to be actually in favour of compulsory Chapel. A voluntary communion service is held before breakfast every Wednesday in the surviving portion of Founder's Chapel.

The playing fields cover 100 acres and form a large part of the estate. Boys are not forbidden to practice golf on them, and perhaps that helped the Old Carthusians to win the Halford Hewitt golf competition (Public School teams) in 1982, 1983 and 1984. Harking further back, one finds that the Old Carthusian team, amateurs of course, won the Football Association Cup in 1881. The pitches are well-drained and are used for hockey, rugby, athletics, tennis, as well as soccer. Tucked among them is a farm where Carthusians do agricultural work. In the woodlands beyond are the purpose-built houses to which parties of primary school children come out from Southwark for a week in the country, hosted by boys and girls. All new boys are taken back to 'Charterhouse in Southwark' to remind them what inner-city life is like and the Mission and Youth Club sponsored by the school is one element of its voluntary Social Service. Scouting still flourishes, with its emphasis on classlessness, internationalism and concern for the handicapped; and one of the school's amenities is Tideswell, in the Derbyshire Peak District, where an old grammar school has been converted to accommodate about thirty Carthusians, as a fine base for field and adventure activities, CCF schemes, archaeological and geographical studies or simply for beaks who want to take a group away for a complete change of environment over a long weekend.

Carthusians are usually questioners, easy to talk to, unselfconscious with strangers or adults, on good terms with their teachers. They tend as much to the Sciences as the Humanities, are culturally sensitive, and are no longer characterized by what Harold Nicholson once described rather unkindly as a 'brash friendliness'. Many parents are not themselves Public School products and the percentage of sons/daughters of OCs is falling, but is still high at

OPPOSITE ABOVE LEFT Calling over 'under the Oak' (*photo Roger Smeeton*)
OPPOSITE ABOVE RIGHT 'Cubes' in one of the old Houses (*photo Roger Smeeton*)
OPPOSITE BELOW Adventure training in the Peak District (*photo Roger Smeeton*)

24 per cent. The majority of them live in Surrey. The Careers Master made a debatable point on the career choices of leavers when he commented that the trend seems to be away from professions that serve the community (armed forces, law, medicine, teaching, etc.) into occupations that exploit it (banking, insurance, etc.). No good Public School produces a 'type'. Among many illustrious OCs are to be found some eccentric personalities – Major-General Orde Wingate, Sir Max Beerbohm, Osbert Lancaster, Richard Murdoch. And in 1984, for the first time, the Lord Mayor of London and both his Sheriffs were from the same old school.

Charterhouse

ADDRESS Godalming, Surrey GU7 2DM

FOUNDATION 1611 by Thomas Sutton

TITLE OF HEAD AND NUMBER OF TEACHING STAFF Head Master + 74
  (excluding visiting teachers)

TOTAL NUMBER OF PUPILS 700

NUMBER IN SIXTH FORM 320

NUMBER OF ADVANCED LEVEL CHOICES AVAILABLE 20

NAMES OF FORMS (i) IVth Form (ii) Remove (iii) Vth Form
  (iv) 1st Year Specialists (v) 2nd Year Specialists

PRINCIPAL GAMES, BY TERMS *Oration* Soccer *Long* Hockey
  Cricket Cricket

NAMES OF HOUSES
In-Houses Saunderites, Verites, Gownboys
Out-Houses Girdlestoneites, Lockites, Weekites, Hodgsonites, Daviesites,
  Bodeites, Pageites, Robinites

APPLICATION AND ENTRY Any time from birth. Preference may be stated
  for a particular House. Entry for boys at 13+, girls at 15/16+

SCHOLARSHIPS, ETC.
At least 12 academic Scholarships of from £500 p.a. to 100% of fees
1 Scholarship of £360 p.a. for Proficiency in Classics
Scholarships in Music and Art available at 13+ and 16+ of from £500 to
  100% of fees
Assisted Places are available for Sixth Form entry

BOOK *A Charterhouse Miscellany* arr. R.L. Arrowsmith

Westminster School

215 BOARDING BOYS
(including 40 Queen's Scholars)
327 DAY BOYS
24 BOARDING GIRLS ⎫ Sixth
60 DAY GIRLS ⎰ Form

AT ABOUT THE SAME TIME AS CHRIST'S HOSPITAL AND CHARTERHOUSE were moving out into the country, the Dean and Chapter suggested that Westminster should do the same, but there was such an uproar of dissent from the boys that the idea was dropped and so, after nearly 1400 years, the school still stands where it has always stood (apart from a period of evacuation during World War II) at the very heart of London. It is a mediaeval school refounded in the sixteenth century and has always been renowned for its scholarship. Today it is unique in the flexibility of its entry arrangements and its blend of boarding, weekly boarding and day pupils, both boys and girls. The buildings, approached through the archway of Dean's Yard, are all within the precincts of Westminster Abbey, an island amidst the swirling currents of London. They are a very mixed lot, following no master plan, but, as the school's historian points out, 'with the incomparable backcloth of the Abbey it would be an impertinence for the school buildings to steal the show'.

The West Minster in the sixth century was one of the principal Benedictine Monasteries in England. It stood in countrified surroundings some miles west of London. Naturally there was a school attached to it. When Henry VIII abolished the Monastery in 1540 he did at least found a grammar school here. Queen Elizabeth I, herself an accomplished scholar, refounded it. That is why to this day there are forty Queen's Scholars. A great Head Master, Dr Richard Busby, ruled for fifty-six years from 1639 to 1695 and put the school on its feet. It nurtured in those days men of the calibre of Locke, Wren and Dryden, and at a later stage more politicians and Prime Ministers even than Eton. The Green Library today contains 700 volumes by 140 Westminsters. No school has educated so many authors of famous and beloved hymns. We have to thank Westminster for George Herbert's 'Let all the World in every corner sing', for Charles Wesley's 'Hark the Herald Angels', for Augustus Toplady's 'Rock of Ages, cleft for me', and many more.

The school shared the vicissitudes of all grammar schools and by the middle of the eighteenth century numbers were down to sixty-seven. Then, as later, there was pressure to move from the contamination of sprawling

Little Dean's Yard with the Victoria Tower of the Houses of Parliament in the background, Ashburnham House, and the Burlington Arch leading to the school (*photo David Herbert*)

London which was now lapping round the precinct. Westminster reaped both the rewards and the penalties of standing its ground. In 1941 fire bombs reduced Christopher Wren's School and College (once the Chapter dormitory) to empty shells. Ashburnham House was partially burned and there was much other damage. In 1945 when the school returned from the country there were only 135 boys. That number has grown with the school's reputation to over 600. How can one account for such success? The site is cramped, the buildings old, there is little scope for expansion, not a playing field in sight, no imposing new classroom block, no sports hall cum swimming pool, no smart new Design and Technology block. The boarding Houses are adaptations of town houses, most grouped round Dean's Yard, and the class-rooms are scattered anonymously among the buildings roundabout. Water-men have to take an Underground to Putney to row on the Tideway, footballers and cricketers have to trudge through streets to Vincent Square and many other sports rely on hired courts and premises. On the other hand, Ashburnham House, whose well-furnished rooms are now available for private study, is a fine example of seventeenth-century architecture. The fourteenth-century College Hall was once the Abbot's state dining-room. School, where all the classes were once held and whose shell-shaped end provided a class name for many other schools (the Shell), was executed by Burlington to a design by Wren. The Head Master's study and the 1650 Busby Library are both fine and inspiring rooms. Close at hand rise the

LEFT Westminsters in front of Ashburnham House with the Abbey behind (*photo Natasha Nicholson*)

RIGHT 1–3 Little Dean's Yard (residence of the Under Master and Grant's and Rigaud's boarding houses) (*photo David Herbert*)

BELOW Little Dean's Yard: the History block and Liddell's Arch (*photo A. Linger*)

Entrance to College Hall (*Westminster School*)

Victoria Tower, Big Ben, and the majestic bulk of Westminster Abbey, and every day every pupil, of *whatever* denomination, attends a service in that awesome interior. The Houses of Parliament across the road are near enough for a two-way traffic – Scholars to listen to debates, Members of both Houses to speak to Societies in the school. But the principal reason for the school's success is its academic excellence, based on the old classical traditions. Westminster's Advanced Level results in 1984 tell their own story. Total number of candidates: 146. Subjects taken: 461. Percentage of passes 98, of which 37 per cent were Grade A. In 1983/4 13 pupils won Awards to Oxbridge.

The principal feature of Westminster is its flexibility. Entry is possible at the age of 10, 13 or 16. Perhaps alone among Public Schools it welcomes boys and Sixth Form girls as day pupils, full boarders or weekly boarders. Weekly boarders are allowed to go home from Saturday afternoon till Monday morning. It is an easy and logical arrangement, especially for London families, enabling parents and children to pursue their own interests during the week

OPPOSITE ABOVE Westminster School. Dean's Yard with Westminster Abbey in the background (*photo David Herbert*)
OPPOSITE BELOW St Paul's School (*photo Harry Sowden*)

Dulwich College

and enjoy each other's company – one hopes – at the weekend. The pastoral system is based on Houses and Housemasters. They are Houses in more than name, for they sit down to eat together in their own dining-rooms and have their own habitation.

There are five boarding Houses, to some of which day-boys may be attached, and three day-boy Houses. Boarders start by having a desk in an open house-room and a bed or bunk in an unpartitioned dormitory. They move up to a shared study by day and a smaller dormitory. These studies usually have three or four desks, one of which may be a day boy's. The Queen's Scholars' house-rooms, which they call Election Rooms, offer greater privacy with their individual cubicles. College is a House on its own, though not a whole separate building, for the forty Queen's Scholars, whose presence does so much to raise the academic level of the whole school. Entry to College is by the Challenge, a special scholarship examination on which ten places a year are awarded. For others there is an interview at the age of 10, and Common Entrance is taken at 13+. Pressure for places means that the entry level is high and this has enabled academic standards to be pushed up. Girls may only enter at Sixth Form level, when some boys are also admitted. All have to sit a Westminster entry examination. In addition there is now a Junior School providing for admission at the age of 10 and progression up through the Lower and Senior Schools.

The type of parent has altered little in a hundred years. Mostly they are the professional people of London with a leavening of self-employed and executives. On the whole they have ridden inflation well, and there is now a new breed, the mother who has a full-time job. The Westminster recipe suits them well and is particularly well-adapted to a city school. Westminster was relatively unaffected by the changes of the mid-nineteenth century and preserved the old eighteenth-century grammar school traditions. It was relatively little affected by the surge of athleticism and 'muscular Christianity' of the Victorian period. Games-playing 'bloods' never reigned supreme here. *The Elizabethan* is concerned more with cultural matters (34 pages) than with sport (5 pages). Even the senior Westminster is reluctant to exercise authority. In fact, elaborate rules had not been found necessary in a fairly relaxed community until the 1980s with their erosion of standards. Tails, top hat and umbrella yielded to black coat and grey trousers after World War II. The Westminster is less insulated from the maturing though sometimes dangerous influence of the outside world than most Public School pupils.

No longer do Westminsters play football in the Cloisters or fight till they drop in Dean's Yard, but they honour many of their old traditions. The Latin play is performed annually as it has been for four centuries. It has been attended by many Princes and four reigning monarchs: Elizabeth I, William IV, George VI and Elizabeth II. The pancake is still tossed over the Greaze Pole in School on Shrove Tuesday – the Pancake Greaze. Every 17 November, anniversary of Elizabeth I's death, the Scholars gather round the tomb where she lies buried upon the anonymous grave of her sister Mary (Bloody Mary).

Regno consortes et urna, hic obdormimus Elizabetha et Maria sorores, in spe resurectionis. Even more memorable to a young person's mind are the great state occasions where Westminsters and Queen's Scholars especially have a privileged place. At the Coronation of the second Elizabeth in 1953 millions of listeners heard the Westminster Scholars proclaim the newly-crowned Sovereign with their adolescent shout of 'Vivat! Vivat Regina! VIVAT! VIVAT!'

Westminster School

ADDRESS Little Dean's Yard, Westminster, London SW1P 3PF

FOUNDATION Refounded 1560 by Queen Elizabeth I

GOVERNING BODY The Governors, Chairman The Dean of Westminster

TITLE OF HEAD AND NUMBER OF TEACHING STAFF Head Master + 52 (excluding visiting teachers)

TOTAL NUMBER OF PUPILS 600

NUMBER IN SIXTH FORM 300

NUMBER OF ADVANCED LEVEL CHOICES AVAILABLE 19

NAMES OF FORMS (i) Transitus (ii) Fifth Form (iii) Lower and Upper Shell (iv) Sixth (v) Remove (vi) Seventh

PRINCIPAL GAMES, BY TERMS *Play* Soccer *Lent* Soccer *Election* Cricket. Rowing throughout the year

NAMES OF HOUSES
Boarding College (Queen's Scholars), Grant's, Rigaud's, Busby's, Liddell's
Day Ashburnham, Wren's, Dryden's

APPLICATION AND ENTRY Registration up to age 10; interview at 10. Entry for boys at 8+ and 10+ to Junior School, 13+ to Lower School; girls 15/16+ to Sixth Form

SCHOLARSHIPS, ETC.
10 Queen's Scholarships of 50% fees (may be augmented up to 100% of fees)
1 Music Scholarship of 50% fees

TOTAL ANNUAL ALLOCATION FOR SCHOLARSHIPS, ETC. £200,000

BOOK *Westminster School* by John Carleton

St Paul's School

122 BOARDING BOYS

679 DAY BOYS

ST PAUL'S IN WEST LONDON IS ONE OF THE OLDEST PUBLIC SCHOOLS and when it was founded as a day school was the largest in the land. Throughout its history it has had a remarkable record of academic excellence and has produced many remarkable men, among them Milton and Pepys, Marlborough and Montgomery.

'John Colet DD 1509 Dean of St Paul's founded and endowed this School in honour of Christ Jesu and of his Blessed Mother Mary for a CLIII boys of all nacions and countres to be taught free in the same in good literature both Laten and Greke.' Colet's father had been a wealthy London Mercer whose only son had entered the priesthood and thus had no heirs. On his death the Dean left both his father's fortune and his own considerable property to found a school, the management of which he handed over to the Mercers' Company. It is believed that he set the number of Scholars at 153 because that was the number of fishes in the Miraculous Draught. The Foundation Scholars of today still wear an emblem of a silver fish. The original school was hard by St Paul's Cathedral but was destroyed, with precious Miltoniana, in the Great Fire of London. In successive moves it slid westward and by 1939 occupied a vast Gothic edifice in West Kensington. When the school was evacuated in World War II this became the Headquarters of General Montgomery's 21 Army Group. Monty was an Old Pauline and it was with relish that he took over a room into which he had never ventured as a boy, the study of the High Master. Here in May 1944 he outlined his plan for the military invasion of France, Overlord, to a gathering which included Churchill and George VI. Later he became a member of the Mercers' Company and took a keen interest in the school's fortunes. Not entirely by coincidence one of his former Liaison Officers, Major T.E.B. Howarth, MC, was High Master in the mid-1960s.

At that time the old Gothic building was becoming a financial burden and the eleven-acre site was both restricted and restrictive. St Paul's needed a lung, but was determined not to move out into the country as Charterhouse and Christ's Hospital had done, but to preserve its urban identity. Fortunately, the London County Council at that time were not hostile, although Socialist. A site was found just west of Hammersmith Bridge on the south bank of the Thames, occupied by fifty acres of redundant Metropolitan Water Board reservoirs. The LCC bought the old School for housing development, and sold St Paul's the fifty acres to be used in a way that could only enhance

The Colet Memorial by Hamo Thornycroft, given to the school in 1902 by
Edward H. Palmer and moved from Hammersmith to the new school at Barnes in 1968
(*photo Walton Adams*)

the environment, a low-profiled school with extensive playing fields. With the million-odd pounds it received for the sale and the proceeds of an Appeal, St Paul's were able to plan the ideal school on the other side of the river, still well within the embrace of London but with all the advantages of a rural setting. The High Master sat down with his architect in front of a blank sheet of paper in the same room where Montgomery had drawn up his plans to cross a more substantial strip of water.

St Paul's is alone among Public Schools in having moved to a purpose-built site where all the requirements of modern education were available, thus remaining one of the oldest schools but becoming one of the most up-to-date. The buildings were constructed on the Clasp system, whereby pre-fabricated concrete and aggregate slabs are hung on beams and present a utilitarian but hard-wearing aspect that makes no brash statement in this architecturally humble environment. There was much glass, and flat roofs were mandatory but the classrooms and corridors were carpeted, a startling innovation at that time. As a Chapel is not so important in a day school, the Library was made the focal point, which is befitting in a school that has produced so many Scholars and men of letters. There was much discussion about how many mementoes of the old school should be moved. Monty told the High Master: 'It doesn't matter about the rest of the stuff so long as you take me and Marlborough'. So the twin portraits of the two great British Generals hang in the Montgomery Room at Barnes, some stained glass adorns the new Assembly Hall, and the statue of John Colet under his wrought-iron canopy greets every visitor who drives up the entrance avenue.

The new site with its forty acres of playing fields makes the running of a day school vastly easier. In the same complex of buildings are the two modern boarding Houses and the preparatory school, Colet Court. St Paul's Girls' School, the sister foundation, is now just that little bit more awkward to reach, which slightly invalidates the reasons given for not admitting girls here – or boys there. As the school has moved westwards its clientele has become more middle-class, though still predominantly the professional people of West London, with boys coming daily from as far away as Stanmore, Guildford and Windsor. The standard of entry is high and all future pupils have to undergo an interview two years before. The award of up to forty Scholarships a year supplies a core of very clever boys, proportionately much more than at Eton or even Winchester. Scholars entering from Colet Court, the preparatory school, have to 'convert' (take the exam) as do those receiving the award in the Sixth Form, here called the Eighth in deference to John Colet's instructions. All Scholarships are paid on a means test, so parents may receive from 15 per cent to 100 per cent of the fees. Colet's school is thus still fulfilling its charitable purpose of providing free or almost free education for those in need.

A factor in the academic success is the very high quality of the staff, attracted not only by the advantages of a London day school but also by the opportunity to teach clever and interesting boys. There is also the tutorial system, introduced in 1968. Masters each have about fifteen boys in three different age-groups whose progress right through the school they watch over with personal interest. Parents are encouraged to invite them to the boys' homes, so that they may become personal friends and also provide a link between school and family. The boarding Housemasters are Tutors to their boys. Tutors have a weekly session with their personal pupils every Monday.

'Laten and Greke' are still taught, no fewer than two dozen taking those subjects at O Level and quite a few going on to do A Level, more doing Latin than Greek in the Eighth Form. But St Paul's is not a school with a Classical emphasis, and boys are free to make their own choice, both for A Level subjects and minority time. The result is a fair balance between the Sciences and Humanities with quite a lot of cross-pollenating. Of the 32 periods a week, A Level work normally takes up 24; four more are spent on General Studies and various options, and four on private study. Senior boys have tiny carrel units where they can put their heads down and work, if they are not using the Library.

They are strongly discouraged from using the lunch break, 12.45–2.40 p.m., for doing homework. This time is preserved for extra-curricular activities, meetings perhaps of some of the thirty-two Societies, or talks from visiting speakers. The results achieved at the end of this sophisticated and highly-tuned academic process surpass those of any other school in the land. St Paul's does not trumpet its A Level results from the flat roof-tops, in fact is modestly secretive about them. All that can be said is that it is very rare for a Pauline to fail any subject at Advanced Level, and of those who pass a high proportion (64 per cent) achieve A or B Grades. Less classified are the figures for entrance and Awards to Cambridge and Oxford. St Paul's can claim over the years to have won more Awards in relation to its size than any other school. Last year fifty-seven Paulines went up to Cambridge and Oxford, twenty of them with Awards, and a Pauline won the top Scholarship in Classics at Corpus Christi, Oxford.

St Paul's is a Rugger school and in the annual fixture against Dulwich no less than a dozen teams participate. The Spring Term is kept for miscellaneous sports and in the Summer time is shared between Cricket and Rowing, the latter being a sport for all seasons. A vast Sports Centre harbours numerous activities, but where St Paul's is pre-eminent is in Tennis, having won the Youll Cup for schools at the All England Club every year from 1976 to 1980.

Paulines are a quixotic and interesting lot who become involved in a fantastic variety of activities. A survey of those who left in 1972 showed the wide range of things they do – from the Church to the Navy, through art dealing,

OPPOSITE ABOVE The inner quadrangle (*photo Walton Adams*)
OPPOSITE BELOW LEFT A history tutorial (*photo Walton Adams*)
OPPOSITE BELOW RIGHT Instructing new boys in the art of sculling
on the River Thames (*photo Walton Adams*)

TV programme research, writing music, information technology. The Old Pauline Club is diversified and lively, one quarter of *The Pauline*'s pages being devoted to its activities.

Old and present Paulines together with parents and well-wishers make a yearly pilgrimage back to St Paul's Cathedral for the Annual Feast Service, to remember their Founder, the central figure among the English humanists and a friend of that great European, Erasmus.

St Paul's School

ADDRESS Lonsdale Road, Barnes, London SW13 9JT

FOUNDATION 1509 by John Colet, Dean of St Paul's Cathedral

GOVERNING BODY Master and Wardens of the Mercers' Company, plus 9 from Oxford, Cambridge and London Universities

TITLE OF HEAD AND NUMBER OF TEACHING STAFF High Master + 65 (excluding visiting teachers)

TOTAL NUMBER OF PUPILS 770

NUMBER IN SIXTH FORM 400 (will become 350)

NUMBER OF ADVANCED LEVEL CHOICES AVAILABLE 23+

NAMES OF FORMS (i) Fourth (ii) Fifth (iii) Sixth (iv) Lower Eighth (v) Middle Eighth (vi) Upper Eighth

PRINCIPAL GAMES, BY TERMS *Autumn* Rugby *Spring* Miscellaneous *Summer* Cricket and Rowing

NAMES OF HOUSES
School is divided into Clubs, not Houses
Boarding Houses High House, School House

APPLICATION AND ENTRY Interview at 11+, entry at 13+

SCHOLARSHIPS, ETC.
35/40 Foundation Scholarships, awarded at age 13+ (Junior) or 16+ (Senior) value from 15% to 100% of tuition fee (means test)
3 Music Scholarships from 15% to 100% tuition fee (means test)
Other Scholarships and Exhibitions and Assisted Places are available

TOTAL ANNUAL ALLOCATION FOR SCHOLARSHIPS, ETC. £300,000 to £450,000

BOOK *St. Paul's School 1909–1959* by F.R. Salter

Dulwich College

EDWARD ALLEYN WAS A THEATRICAL VENTURER WHO BUILT THE Fortune Theatre in Elizabethan London and in the reign of James I became Master of the Royal Game of Bears, Bulls and Mastiff dogs. He was rich enough to buy the Manor and 1500 acres at Dulwyche, a village to the south-east of London. He may have acquired his wealth by dubious means but he used it to make a charitable foundation, his 'College of God's Gift'. The foundation embraces three schools with a total of 2,700 boys and girls: Alleyn's School, James Allen's Girls' School and Dulwich College. Today this last is one of the great London day schools, serving the whole south-east area. That there was little change at Dulwich for two hundred years was emphasized by the fact that the first half-dozen headmasters had to adopt the name Alleyn, and though the Fellows were Royalist, they survived the Civil War. Then two great advances in communications made Dulwich fashionable. By 1820 the roads had been macadamized and the carriage-borne gentry built villas here. In 1851 the Crystal Palace, home of the Great Exhibition, had been moved from Hyde Park to Sydenham Hill, and in the 1860s three railway companies bought land from the College for lines from London to Chatham, Dover and Brighton. Dulwich was now a Public School and this new wealth enabled a more modern college to be built, in the Italian style, which was opened by the Prince of Wales in 1870. A.H. Gilkes, Master from 1885 to 1914, laid the foundations of the modern school. Among his pupils was Ernest Shackleton, one of whose books, printed in the Antarctic and bound with wood from a tea chest, is preserved in the Archives. Another was P.G. Wodehouse, who left in 1900. He must have been happy here for even at the age of 30 he would come back to watch Rugger matches, tearing up and down the touchline to encourage the Alleynians. His study, exactly as he left it with spectacles and all, is preserved behind glass in the modern library. The complete set of P.G. Wodehouse's works collected by Barry Phelps makes Dulwich College the definitive place for Wodehouse scholars.

In 1914 the regulations required all boys over 14 to join the Officers Training Corps, and all seniors to spend ten hours a week training. On leaving they were commissioned in the OTC and sent straight out to France as subalterns. It was calculated that at one time the average expectation of life of a lieutenant in action was twenty minutes. Of 3,036 Alleynians who served in 1914–18, 506 were killed and 5 won VCs. Twenty-one years later the next generation was again offered as a sacrifice, 330 being killed, with two more

VCs and a George Cross. Dulwich was the only London school which continued to work above ground from 1939 to 1945 under bombs, V1s and V2s,
though south-east London was the main point of impact for the rockets.
(The reason why is explained in *Most Secret War* by R.V. Jones, an OA.)

The post-war years from 1945 onwards saw an experiment of extraordinary
social and educational interest at the College. Under the Education Act of
1944 any child who passed the Common Entrance exam of his local authority
qualified for a free place at an independent secondary day school, the authority
paying the fees. The then Master, C.H. Gilkes, opened his door not only to
the London County Council but to other local authorities, and so began the
Dulwich Experiment. Numbers expanded rapidly from 400 to 1,000. In
1946 one quarter of the school were new boys, from local authority schools in

View through main gate (*Dulwich College*)

Main buildings (*Dulwich College*)

London, Surrey and Kent. Dulwich had the pick of the field, to the chagrin of the London grammar schools and the political Left. Nor were the Old Alleynians too pleased at this change in the character of the school. By 1951 two out of three applicants were being turned away and the school's finances were on a sound basis. New building was undertaken, notably a Science Block, perhaps the best in the country. By the mid-fifties 86 per cent of the boys were local authority Scholars and Dulwich had become a super grammar school. Between 1966 and 1976 more Awards to Cambridge and Oxford were won than by any other school, and with a very wide spread in the subjects studied. Clever boys attract brilliant teachers and the quality of the staff rose steadily. A job at an academic day school on the outskirts of London had much attraction. When school ended and boys went home, masters were free to pursue their own interests. They were not as involved as boarding-school masters in the minutiae of pastoral care; they were more in contact with the outside world and the life of the metropolis, and brought some of that stimulation back into their classrooms. In 1964 the Master wrote: 'If there is anything in this idea of integrating schools into the State system Dulwich has tried to do it and be fair to everybody'. But already the LCC were reducing the numbers they were sending and other local authorities gradually followed suit. The era of the Comprehensive School was dawning. A plan was mooted for a degree of integration with the five comprehensive schools which surrounded the College, but it came to nothing and a unique opportunity was lost. By 1965 the Labour Government was pledged 'to reduce the socially divisive influence of the Public Schools'. Gradually the number of boys aided by local authorities declined until by 1978 there was none left. The Dulwich Experiment was over.

Of course it had been élitist but only in an academic sense. Most of the parents concerned were skilled artisans, with a smaller number of manual workers, shopkeepers and, interestingly, policemen. The fathers as a whole represented a cross-section of south-east London and a wider spectrum of society than any other school. When the scheme was killed by politicians, the Governors realized that if poorer families were to be helped it would have to be from the Foundation's own resources. In 1971 eight new scholarships

Old Time Tuition at Dulwich College, by J.C. Horsley, 1828 (*Dulwich Picture Gallery*)

The P.G. Wodehouse Memorial Study in the Wodehouse Library (*Dulwich College*)

were established, bringing the total up to twenty a year. When the Conservative Government introduced its Assisted Places Scheme, funded centrally, the College decided to offer fifty places and also to increase its own bursaries. By 1984 a total of forty scholarships and exhibitions was available.

Dulwich College today caters for 1,380 boys, of whom 140 are boarders. They work a five-day week from 8.50 a.m. till 3.40 p.m., with voluntary activities after that and at the weekend. The Lower School teaches boys aged 8 to 13, with special emphasis on English and Mathematics. In the Middle School a wide variety of courses leads to Ordinary Level in from eight to eleven subjects. In the Upper School three or four Advanced Levels are taken from a range of twenty subjects. Over-specialization is prevented by an imaginative selection of General Studies and by seventeen different Options. 'Cast around and risk some adventure', the notice exhorts pupils. Sixth Formers not doing A Level English must do two periods of English a week and one period of Religious Studies. This brings the number of periods spent on non-examinable subjects to seven a week, and the deliberate broadening of the curriculum seems if anything to enhance Advanced Level performance. Last year the pass rate was 95 per cent, a score of 3.4. In fifteen out of the twenty-four subjects taken 100 per cent of candidates passed. The fruits of the Dulwich Experiment were richest in the period 1966 to 1981 when Awards won at Cambridge and Oxford averaged 27 per annum and places gained at those Universities averaged 42 per annum. In 1983 a record number, 253, applied for University; 162 were accepted by 33 different Universities. Of these pupils 33 intended to take degrees in Engineering.

The 1,380 boys are divided into eight Houses. They remain in the same House throughout their time, but have a different Housemaster in the Lower, Middle and Upper School. House divisions are mainly for games purposes, though the old name Athletic House has died out. There are also boarding Houses, two for the Lower School and one each for the Middle and Upper, providing for full and weekly boarding, but these are purely residential units.

The primacy of the athletic bloods has disappeared, though games are still compulsory for the Lower School twice a week. The Captain of the School heads a numerous but humane cadre of thirteen Senior Prefects and eighty-five Prefects, and enjoys the use not only of an office but also a waiting-room.

Vacancies occur for boys aged 8, 9, 10, 11 and 13, and selection for entry is academically competitive but regardless of race or creed. Most boys appear to be happy here and OAs usually have affectionate memories of their old school. With the school functioning only seven hours out of twenty-four for only five days a week they have a full life off the school premises. They have no doubt that they are better off here than their contemporaries at the boarding schools they visit, whom they see as somewhat archaic and inward-looking.

Dulwich is unique in possessing its own picture gallery one and a half miles down College Road. The Dulwich Gallery is one of the finest small collections in Europe, with delicious examples of Gainsborough, Poussin, Canaletto, Rubens, Raphael, Tiepolo and Murillo.

The Dulwich Picture Gallery in the 1880s (*Dulwich College*)

Dulwich College

ADDRESS London SE21 7LD

FOUNDATION 1619 by Edward Alleyn

TITLE OF HEAD AND NUMBER OF TEACHING STAFF Master + 109
(excluding visiting teachers)

TOTAL NUMBER OF PUPILS 1,380

NUMBER IN SIXTH FORM 416

NUMBER OF ADVANCED LEVEL SUBJECTS AVAILABLE 22

NAMES OF FORMS *Lower School* First and Second Forms *Middle School*
Third, Fourth and Fifth Forms *Upper School* Removes, Sixth Forms,
Upper Sixths

PRINCIPAL GAMES, BY TERMS *Michaelmas* Rugby *Lent* Hockey   *Summer*
Cricket

NAMES OF HOUSES
Drake, Grenville, Howard, Jonson, Marlowe, Raleigh, Sidney, Spenser.
Boarding only Bell, Orchard, Ivyholme, Blew

APPLICATION AND ENTRY Entry at age 8, 9, 10, 11, 13 and 16. Registration
as long as possible beforehand

SCHOLARSHIPS, ETC.
40 Scholarships and Bursaries of from £450 to £2,595 (full fees) p.a.
2 Music Scholarships of 50% of fees
1 Art Scholarship of 50% of fees
Assisted Places are available

TOTAL ANNUAL ALLOCATION FOR SCHOLARSHIPS, ETC. £200,000

BOOK *God's Gift* by Sheila Hodges

Cheltenham College

380 BOARDING BOYS

140 DAY BOYS

22 DAY GIRLS (Sixth Form)

COLLEGE LIES WITHIN THE EMBRACE OF THE SPA TOWN OF Cheltenham in Gloucestershire, rubbing shoulders with well-favoured private houses. Traffic pulses on the roads that surround it. The main buildings of Cotswold stone enclose the square Green on two sides, giving a collegiate tone to the whole area, and the boarding Houses, mostly of brick, are tucked away in the surrounding built-up area. Geographically, Cheltenham is well placed for Gloucestershire parents, but the nearby M5 extends the catchment area to the South Midlands and South Wales. College has always had strong links with the East, especially Malaysia, and fifty or sixty boys now in the school are from expatriate families.

Cheltenham was the first of seven English Public Schools founded between 1840 and 1850, early in the reign of Queen Victoria. Dr Arnold had been in charge of Rugby for twelve years now and there was a demand for places in Public Schools from the class made affluent by the Industrial Revolution. In the nineteenth century the idea of a Proprietary School was popular. Shares in the College were held by 650 people, each entitled to nominate one pupil. The aim was 'to provide an efficient course of education for the sons of gentlemen', largely retired Colonial servants. An immediate success, it was soon a leading source for the military academies of Sandhurst and Woolwich. By 1880 it was the second largest Public School and numbered as one of ten Great Schools. Many Cheltonians went to serve the Empire in India, thus establishing its connection with the East. In World War I 675 OCs sacrificed their lives, in World War II the number was 347. The VC has been awarded to fourteen OCs, almost the highest tally of any school. The first Field-Marshal was Sir John Dill and the most recent hero Major-General Sir Jeremy Moore, OBE, MC, of the Falklands Task Force. Cheltenham has also produced its authors, including Nobel Prize winner Patrick White and 'Sapper' (H.C. McNeile); and Dr Edward Wilson of the Antarctic, whose skis lean casually against the wall of the Headmaster's study, was also here. Lindsay Anderson is an OC and, amazingly, was allowed to make his film *If* here. As this was a cruel parody of Public School life it took Cheltenham several years to restore its image.

During the first hundred years there had naturally been changes and additions to College buildings, for those who planned the College in 1840 had been looking to the past rather than the future. At first all teaching was done in two huge rooms, Big Classical and Big Modern. Over the years the former became an assembly hall and the latter a library housing most of the 70,000 books. The original chapel, having served for a time as a museum, is now a superb dining hall. The new Chapel, dedicated in 1896, is a particularly fine edifice with a challenging reredos. The Sports Hall and Pavilion with their Gothic windows and spires remain temples to physical fitness. The Centenary Building of 1939, the gift of OCs and friends, contains thirteen classrooms, one for each of the VCs won by that date. Beside every dais is a framed portrait, with the citation telling how the award was won. The original Victorian school block with its distinctive tower has been partly obscured by later buildings, private as well as collegiate. Some of the former have been acquired by the school, notably the new Arts Centre, and Chandos Lodge, where the twenty-two day girls attending A Level courses have their own centre.

When Cheltenham outgrew its strongly military identity and the ideal of service to the Empire became outmoded, no new inspiration was found. From 1932 until the late seventies College steadily fell behind the other Great Schools. The past six years have been a period of refurbishment, re-building, renewal and the discovery of a fresh direction. A new Headmaster was appointed in 1978 and seventy per cent of the staff have been taken on in the last five years. By 1985 all the Housemasters were recent appointments and there were twelve new heads of department. An Appeal launched in 1977 reached £335,000 by 1983. This has enabled new entry Scholarships to be offered and has fuelled the on-going development plan, which has included modernization of all the boarding Houses, a new boat house, art school, design and technology centre and Science block.

Science has always been important here, especially Biology, thanks to the inspiration of Dr Edward Wilson. The new 14-lab building, as up-to-date and well-equipped as that of any school, has given it a fresh impetus. In the Common Entrance exam there is a scholarship specifically for Science. The Science staff of fifteen are full-time in their own subjects and two of them have been to the Antarctic. Physics, Chemistry and Biology are taught to all boys up to O Level. At least half the Sixth Form are doing a minimum of one Science subject for A Level, and of those the majority are doing more than one.

A new thrust has been in Electronics, which is superseding engineering. The new Electronics Lab is perhaps the most advanced in the UK. Here the 'Cheltenham 11–13 Electronics Board' is produced for use by other schools, as well as many aids for the handicapped made possible by technology. The Technology Centre is at its busiest during free time when eighty to a hundred enthusiasts can be found building their own computers or making devices designed by themselves in the Design Workshop. Art has become much more important in the curriculum since 1980, when space was limited and only the least able boys did Art. Now in the recently acquired classical mansion, former home of a rich collector, a new art centre with generous space

The Tower Entrance, Bath Road (*Cheltenham College*)

and light is opening up. In their first year all boys do the various art subjects and in their second year choose which they will do for O Level. By the mid-1980s, twenty boys were preparing to take A Level Art.

The very wide-awake careers organization reinforces the drive to produce school-leavers geared to the needs of the modern world. Each House has a careers tutor and hosts an outside speaker every term. This encourages boys to relate their O and A Level choices to future employment. A Link Scheme involves boys in the Lower Sixth, fifty or sixty of whom come back five days before the beginning of term and go to a local firm or factory for direct experience. In addition all pupils are given interview experience by undergoing a mock interview with a local firm, when they provide a curriculum vitae and receive a frank report. College runs its own company, Young Enterprise, which carries out research and development. Using the Technology Centre it has produced teaching modules for other schools, a light-pen for use with computers and a personal accounting system.

College today makes a virtue of being part of Cheltenham and forges two-way links with the town. The Science laboratories are available to local schools, the art galleries to local artists, the concert rooms to local groups, and during the Festival Gloucestershire play cricket on the Green. In the other direction about two hundred pupils spend every Wednesday afternoon

Sixth-Form marine ecology (*photo C. Rouan*)

ABOVE Biology field-work
(*photo C. Rouan*)
RIGHT Physics project work
(*photo C. Rouan*)

doing community service in Cheltenham and Upper College pupils are freely allowed down town.

The allocation of Scholarships has quintupled in recent years. Potential in candidates is looked at as much as present performance. Assisted Places are not offered, in deference to the local Maintained Schools. But many Cheltenham mothers go out to work so that they can send their sons to the school as day boys. Day boys have to arrive early for the ten-minute service in the Chapel with which every day begins. Though this is compulsory, the majority of pupils both old and young are in favour. They value the opportunity for quiet and reflection at the start of each school day, and perhaps acquire the capacity to close their ears to what they do not want to hear.

Cheltenham College

ADDRESS Bath Road, Cheltenham GL53 7LD

FOUNDATION 1841 (proprietary)

GOVERNING BODY The Council

TITLE OF HEAD AND NUMBER OF TEACHING STAFF Headmaster + 50 (excluding visiting teachers)

TOTAL NUMBER OF PUPILS 550

NUMBER IN SIXTH FORM 230

NUMBER OF ADVANCED LEVEL CHOICES AVAILABLE 17

NAMES OF FORMS (i) 3rd Form (ii) 4th Form (iii) 5th Form (iv) Lower 6th (v) Upper 6th

PRINCIPAL GAMES, BY TERMS *Winter* Rugby *Spring* Hockey *Summer* Cricket and Rowing

NAMES OF HOUSES
Boarding Boyne, Cheltondale, Christown, Hazelwell, Leconfield, Newick
Day Boys: Southwood, Wilson. Girls: Chandos

APPLICATION AND ENTRY Registration at any time; House preference may be stated. Entry at age 13 to 14

SCHOLARSHIPS, ETC.
1 of up to 80% of fees
4 of up to 50% of fees
2 of up to 25% of fees
5 of up to 20% of fees
Music and Art Awards of up to 40% are available as well as other Bursaries

TOTAL ANNUAL ALLOCATION FOR SCHOLARSHIPS, ETC. £20,000

BOOK *Cheltenham College* by M.C. Morgan

Marlborough College

760 BOARDING BOYS
100 BOARDING GIRLS (Sixth Form)

MARLBOROUGH STANDS ON A SITE IN WILTSHIRE WHOSE HISTORY goes back centuries before the Romans. The Mound that rises among its buildings is as old as its near neighbour Silbury, though only half as high. According to legend it was the burial place of Merlin. William the Conqueror built one of his castles here, for not only did its position have the tactical advantage of commanding the route westward from London but it also enjoyed the amenities of Savernake Forest, the Kennet Valley and the Marlborough Downs. St Anselm came here when he was Archibishop of Canterbury, thus providing a mystical link with Harrow-on-the-Hill. The castle was frequented by kings for two hundred years. Henry II and Henry III spent Christmas here, in 1164 and 1220 respectively, and John slept 135 nights in Marlborough Castle. After 1296 it became a dower of the royal consort. In the fourteenth century it fell into ruin, though the old moat and duelling ground can still be seen. From 1620 to 1750 it belonged to the Seymour family, who built a mansion where the castle had stood; the present New Court was once their stable yard. The drawing-room of Lady Hertford is now part of the masters' Common Room. Named the Adderley Room it contains the largest Gainsborough in England. From 1751 to 1842 the premises became the Castle Inn 'for the Accommodation of the Nobility', and in 1843 it changed hands for the last time.

In 1843, two years after the foundation of Cheltenham, the Great Schools were still only ten in number. Those who could afford it were able to receive education locally in grammar schools, but there was still no State system of education. In that year, however, the government was introducing a Bill to establish, for the first time, a system of elementary schooling for all the nation's children. The notion of the English 'Public School', as later conceived, had not yet come into being and the Reverend Charles Plater was regarded as a bold innovator when he decided to found a school that would be entirely boarding. Two-thirds of the boys would be the sons of clergy and they would pay 60 per cent of the fees paid by laymen. The foundation was incorporated by Royal Charter in 1845 and again in 1853 and 1858. This new idea caught on and within five years numbers had grown to 500. The masters, mostly clergy, were inexperienced and the boys soon got out of hand, becoming a menace to both staff and neighbourhood. The canings and other harsh methods used to deal with the situation led to the 'rebellion' of 1851, and the departure of the Master.

The man brought in to succeed him was G.E.L. Cotton. He came from Rugby and was probably the 'grave young master' of *Tom Brown's School-days*. In his six years as Master he got the school under control and set it on the path for the future. He was the first Headmaster to see that organized games could provide an outlet for youthful energies and offer an alternative to fighting, poaching and vandalism. He appointed masters who played games and let them lead the boys in manly sports. In those days games were played in ordinary clothes and we have a delightful picture of an enthusiastic young master piling into the rugby scrimmage in his top hat. A modern scion of that lineage was Dave Whitaker, the Marlborough master who coached the medal-winning British Amateur Hockey Team in the 1984 Olympics.

The tradition of athleticism once established dies hard. It was not till the Mastership of John Dancy, 1961–72, that Marlborough again became the most innovative of Public Schools. His approach was radical. He abolished disciplinary caning by senior boys, he mitigated inter-House rivalry by reducing the importance of games and he did away with compulsory daily Chapel. On the academic side, Marlborough helped to pioneer Nuffield Science and the Schools Mathematical Project. The College was perhaps the first to introduce a Business Studies Course, and to make its premises available for a Summer School; 500 people of all ages and all walks of life come in the summer holidays to follow a wide range of residential courses. Three

(*photo David Herbert*)

LEFT Rugby match on Level Broadleaze (*photo John Powell*)
RIGHT Returning from public examinations in the Town Hall (*photo John Powell*)

generations of a family can be represented and you might find a lathe operator buying a drink for the Chairman of the Dublin Stock Exchange from the Housemaster behind the bar.

Of all Dancy's innovations the most startling was to start admitting girls into the Sixth Form. Girls in an English Public School! In 1968 it rocked the dovecotes. Since then many schools have followed suit, even become co-educational, and there are now nearly 100 girls at Marlborough. They are divided up among the boarding Houses, about half a dozen to each. They have studies alongside the boys but sleep separately, usually above the House-master's rooms. Most find the transition to a male-dominated society diffi-cult and may be a little discountenanced when subjected to the Marlborough tradition of a ducking in a cold bath on your birthday. There is also an element of stress involved in being a minority – either shunned if one is plain or too much in demand if one is attractive. Every morning the Master's wife presides over 'girls' break', when for half an hour they can let their hair down and be all girls together. One effect of this influx is that the Sixth Form numbers 420 and comprises half the school. The girls are also credited with having had a 'civilizing' effect on what was previously a very communal society. Competition for places is keen. Girls are carefully selected with an eye on their ability to stand up to the rigours of the Sixth Form in a boys' Public School.

Today Marlborough is a liberal school where more than in most Public Schools there is mixing 'twixt Houses, age-groups, boys and girls, pupils and teachers. Yet even today two currents are apparent. On the one hand there is the undertow of the old Victorian tradition, and on the other the groundswell of liberalism. This is a place where some dishevelment in the physical and sartorial sense is counterbalanced by a burgeoning of the spirit. The original architectural plan still greatly influences the actual organization of the school. From the very beginning all the boys had meals in a central dining-room – a feature widely imitated in recent decades. The Norwood Dining Hall, commemorating a great Master, was rebuilt in 1962. It can seat the whole school for lunch. There are House tables, but the kind of mixing referred to above is allowed.

There are two categories of boarding Houses. The ten original Victorian In-College Houses were built around the spacious Court, the heart of the school. They are arranged in pairs like Siamese twins, and are unromantically named A1, A2, etc. They have broad parquet-floored corridors with shiny brick walls. Boys spend one year in a junior House. In the senior Houses they move up from partitioned spaces in study-rooms to individual bed-sitters. Turner House is the only In-College all-age House. The girls' day studies are shared between four or five and are decorated with pin-ups of, say, James Dean, David Bowie and the pristine Sean Connery. The six Out-College Houses are all-age and flank the Bath Road to the west. Their occupants start in large rooms divided into living and sleeping areas. In the former they have a desk enclosed by a 4-foot partition and in the latter a bed-space similarly enclosed. In their second year they share a study by day and sleep in a dormitory. Sixth Formers have their own bed-sitters. Out-College boys and girls have breakfast and sometimes supper in their Houses. Every House has its Housemaster and one resident Tutor. Other teachers are also attached as Tutors and any evening there may be half a dozen, men and women, going round to give friendly help and advice. Heads of Houses and House Captains, who may be girls, help in running and controlling these small communities.

The teaching staff as a whole are referred to as 'Common Room'. In addition to the gracious Adderley Room they enjoy a dining-room where tea may be taken by all and dinner by those not otherwise provided for. A proper bar adjoins the Bin Room where beaks collect their mail and scribble messages at communal desks.

Marlborough masters pioneered the Business Studies Advanced Level course. Until 1983 Engineering attracted the biggest number of Marlburians going on to degree courses, but in that year Business Studies took the lead, seventy pupils receiving conditional offers to read Business Studies, Management Sciences or Economics at sixteen different Universities. The department now has a new home in the low-built brick Heywood Block and of course it has its own computer. Word-processors and computers are available throughout the school. In one room which is constantly open there are eight terminals geared for word-processing. Quite young boys pop in to put their notes on the word processors and senior boys use them for entire reports or bigger projects. A new Technology Centre is being built around the old chemistry block, which cannot be demolished as it is a Protected Building. In the meantime a Project Laboratory enables Remove boys to sort out a practical problem for themselves, or Sixth Formers to do a one-term Ordinary Level course in control electronics or micro-processing.

Counterbalancing Business and Science is a remarkable Art Department. When a new Art School was built it was deliberately placed in the centre of the school, on the west side of Court, hard by the Dining Hall. In the past twenty years it has become central in more than the geographical sense. No less than six beaks work there. All boys do Art for their first two years and many continue. The Art School is open every single day, as well as three nights a week till 9.30. About fifty boys a year take Ordinary Level, but it is

The Art School (*photo Simon Brett*)

as an Advanced Level and Degree subject that Art has proved its worth. About 100 Sixth Formers do Art A Level, though surprisingly only a quarter of the girls make that choice. In recent years over 90 per cent of candidates obtained Grade A or B, and up to two dozen a year have gone on to read for Art degrees. This makes it the biggest degree subject in the school. A Grade A in Art can be a decisive element in getting a place, for when a candidate has taken four Advanced Levels universities will consider his or her best three subjects.

Another building which was placed in a dominant position stands rather forlornly opposite the Gate Sergeant's Lodge. The Chapel of St Michael and All Angels, built 1883–6, is an example of the English decorated manner. Its dark mysterious Gothic style suited the high-church tone of Marlborough's early years better than the liberal mood of today. It is easy to abolish compulsory Chapel and very difficult to re-impose it, even if you want to. Today only first-year boys have compulsory services, three times a week. For the

The College First Orchestra rehearsing in the Memorial Hall (*photo Jolyon Rugewell*)

rest there is compulsion only on Sundays, when they can choose between a religious service and a Talk. About 100–150 choose the service. Religious Education, however, is compulsory for all, and the emphasis has not changed all that much. The spirit which sent earlier Marlburians into the Church, the Armed Forces or foreign service directs their modern counterparts into fields where they can contribute to society in a different way – into medicine, teaching, engineering or management. Two or three a year still go on to read Theology at University. Of the 200 who leave each year, 150 or so go on to degree courses. Figures for the years 1966 and 1983 showed how emphasis has shifted from Cambridge and Oxford to provincial Universities, as well as the increased overall entry to Universities:

Year	Total leavers	Cambridge and Oxford	Other Universities	All Universities
1966	196	26.5%	21%	47.5%
1983	191	14.7%	52.4%	67.1%

The careers advice service is particularly active and efficient. The University/Careers centre issues weekly bulletins for the use of Housemasters as well as pamphlets and leaflets on such problems as choosing a career, dealing with the UCCA form, handling an interview. A computer terminal, available to any pupil who walks in, gives him or her direct access to the ISCO (Independent Schools Career Organization) service or a read-out on each of forty different careers. The policy is not to confront pupils suddenly with the problem of What next? but to provoke thought and provide information on a structural basis.

Marlborough in the 1980s is open, free and airy, with its expansive grassed courts and lawns enclosed by brick buildings of a reassuring roseate hue. Its entrance gates open at the end of the market town's broad main street, the Parish Church forming a link between town and gown. Old Marlburians remain faithful to the College; about 30 per cent of entrants have OM fathers, largely from business and professional classes, the clergy being especially favoured. Mixed with this old guard is an increasing number of non-Public School parents, themselves the products of grammar schools, but there are few 'City' fathers. One parent, a Welshman, had taken a job in Dubai so that he could send his son to Marlborough, because at his local school Physics was taught in Welsh. The bulk of pupils live below a line from the Mersey to the Wash, but the catchment area for girls is wider.

Where tradition survives at Marlborough it is in modern dress. The House Shout was a ritual, held in the colonnaded War Memorial Hall, when each House put on some kind of choral performance. The boys and girls have put pep into the old tradition and made it swing, dressing up and staging chorus routines of the *Guys and Dolls* style. It is all very different from the environment which Siegfried Sassoon found 'mentally unprofitable' and where a bewildered John Betjeman was *Summoned by Bells*.

Marlborough College

ADDRESS Marlborough, Wiltshire SN8 1PA

FOUNDATION 1843 by the Reverend Charles Plater

GOVERNING BODY The Council (9 Clergy and 14 laymen)

TITLE OF HEAD AND NUMBER OF TEACHING STAFF Master + 90 (excluding visiting teachers)

TOTAL NUMBER OF PUPILS 860

NUMBER IN SIXTH FORM 420

NUMBER OF ADVANCED LEVEL CHOICES AVAILABLE 20

NAMES OF FORMS (i) Shell (ii) Remove (iii) Hundred (iv) Lower Sixth (v) Sixth (vi) Upper Sixth

PRINCIPAL GAMES, BY TERMS *Michaelmas* Rugby *Lent* Hockey *Summer* Cricket

NAMES OF HOUSES
In-College Junior A1, A2, Elmhurst
In-College Senior B1, B2, B3, C1, C2, C3
In-College all-age Turner
Out-College all-age Preshute, Littlefield, Cotton House, Summerfield, Barton Hill

APPLICATION AND ENTRY Registration from birth. Entry at 13+ for boys and 16+ for girls and a few boys

SCHOLARSHIPS, ETC.
2 Scholarships of 70% of fees
12 Scholarships and Exhibitions of 20% + according to means
Closed Awards to Anglican Clergy and HM Forces, of £150 to £650 p.a.
2 Art Scholarships of up to 50% fees
4 Music Scholarships
6 Scholarships for Sixth Form entry: 4 academic, 1 Art, 1 Music

TOTAL ANNUAL ALLOCATION FOR SCHOLARSHIPS ETC. £289,000

BOOK *Marlborough College: A short History and Guide* by Simon Brett

Radley College

RADLEY BECAME KNOWN TO MILLIONS OF VIEWERS WHEN IT WAS featured in the television documentary-serial *Public School*. The TV team spent a year at the College, filming the formal and informal aspects of life there. The informality was sometimes exaggerated, even distorted, to make an episode amusing. But it did give the general public some idea of what happens beyond the gates of a Public School.

It was an act of trust on the part of the Warden to allow the film to be made, and was in line with his statement, 'our aim is to share rather than exclude'. The College makes many of its facilities available to the local community. The running track has been used for ten years by the Radley Ladies Athletic Club and has helped them to climb into the Premier Division. Local children use the Gym and learn to swim in the pool under the eye of the College Porter, a cross-Channel swimmer. The village cricket team play on a Radley wicket, the police and rifle club use the shooting range, and locals play squash and tennis on the courts. During the summer holidays young footballers come in groups of 200 for a week's coaching; they sleep in dormitories and eat in Hall. Now, local golfers can play on the new 9-hole course.

St Peter's College takes its name from the village of Radley, seven miles south of Oxford, two miles north of Abingdon and a couple of miles west of the Thames. The 500-acre park is on elevated ground and the College buildings have grown up round the Mansion which was built in 1720 for Sir John Stonehouse. There is space for all the staff to be accommodated within the Park, and as you drive in you see miniature housing estates tucked among the trees. In contrast to Marlborough, Radley has no central quadrangle or complex of original buildings. When the Reverend William Sewell founded the school in 1847 he leased the Mansion and for some time it contained the whole school. It survives intact, a fine example of eighteenth-century architecture with a strictly symmetrical facade, mellow brickwork and restrained decoration in stone. Early on, of course, he built a Chapel, for he was another dedicated founder of boarding schools with a strong Church of England emphasis. Other early additions were the Dormitory, the Octagon (in fact a decagon) and the Cloisters, now Covered Passage. Sewell gave Radley three other extremely unusual buildings. The first was a bell tower, which he deemed essential in a school. Later, buttresses were extended from the four corners to create quaint fives courts, and a clock was installed. This quirky tower is the focal point of the College. Then he acquired an old half-timbered oak barn and had it rebuilt on the site as a temporary Schoolroom; it still

School, Clock Tower and the Old Gymnasium (now used as a theatre)
(*photo P.L. Kilsby*)

serves a useful purpose. Thirdly, he got onto a firm that built corrugated iron churches for export to Australia, intercepted one and had it erected as a gymnasium - probably the second school gym in England. It now serves as a theatre, the corrugated iron having been replaced by modern material. His Chapel was replaced in the 1890s by a neo-perpendicular building which also had inward-facing pews. It contains a fine Flemish oak altar-piece, *circa* 1510-15. The Chapel, opening off Covered Passage, is still at the heart of the school, as Sewell intended.

The boarding Houses are here called Socials. There are four Out-College Socials in detached houses and four In-College Socials which are in the main complex of buildings. They are named prosaically A to H, and the number of boys in each ranges from seventy-one to seventy-seven. The housemaster is called a Social Tutor, and is usually assisted by another resident 'Don', by a Matron and perhaps also by a wife. In a typical Social, Stigs (new boys) spend their first year in a Social Hall, a big room where each has a 'horse-box' (personal partitioned desk), and sleep in a large open dormitory. In the second year they move into a shared study and sleep in a cubicle with a wash-basin and radiator. There are spacious TV rooms, libraries and areas for socializing.

The classrooms vary in style and quality. Some of them are rather basic and one group is known affectionately as 'the Slums'. Departments are grouped geographically, with Modern Languages, History, Classics, Divinity, and Business Studies in the main building. English, Maths and Geography

The Memorial Arch built *c*.1920 to commemorate casualties of World War I. The Chapel of the Resurrection is above the arch (*photo P.L. Kilsby*)

have more lowly buildings of a somewhat temporary nature. They do have pleasant interiors and good outlooks over the playing fields that surround the school on all sides. If it is easy to find fault with the architectural merit of some classrooms it is harder to fault the teaching that is given inside them. The academic standard is pushed up by the generous number of Scholars. Until 1984 they were put in a fast stream that took them to Ordinary Level in two years. But it is considered unwise to push pupils on to Advanced Level before they are mature and now the Scholars also have a three-year approach to O Level. However, they are setted in certain subjects and may take O Level a year early in Latin, Maths and English. All first-year boys do a Classical Civilization course and can then choose whether to continue Classics or start a second Modern Language. A combined Science course in the lower school embraces Physics, Chemistry and Biology and leads to two O Levels. All boys go through the crafts centre and can pick a subject to take to O Level. In the Fifth Form about 110 candidates take 18 subjects at O Level, obtaining about 94 per cent passes.

When it comes to choosing Advanced Level subjects the school divides about equally between the Humanities and Science. Boys are not encouraged to combine the two. In any given year you would find five boys doing Greek A Level and about fifteen doing Latin. History has a strong tradition, but English is now rivalling it. The number doing Maths and Science is almost a hundred. Every department at Radley has taught up to Oxbridge entry and

Croome's Arch and Tower, 1906 (Paton's Quad) (*photo P.L. Kilsby*)

Award standard. In 1984 Awards were won in Classics, Modern Languages, English (2), Metallurgy, History, Mathematics (2), Geography, Engineering, History of Art. The suppression of 'the seventh term', for boys staying on to take the Oxbridge entrance examinations, would be a serious loss here as elsewhere, for it promotes scholarship in the pupils and is stimulating for teachers. Curiously the two great Universities appear to be more ambivalent about academic excellence than most Public Schools. Science has been given a big fillip by the new building, opened in October 1984 by Margaret Thatcher. It has modern facilities so sophisticated that they baffle the layman, though we can boggle at the notion of boys measuring the speed of light. Radley does not use the Nuffield courses, preferring a theoretical and rationalistic approach to the more traditional one of 'experiment, measure, observe'. The new laboratories are reminiscent of Shrewsbury's – on one side a lecture/demonstration area with a tiered auditorium and, on the other, space for practical work. Thus teacher and class can move rapidly from one to the other. The Science block has a good library, a computer classroom, an electronics room and a big lecture theatre.

To prevent over-specialization there is a programme of additional subjects which occupies five periods a week. The 'Cultural Cabaret' enables Dons to come up with courses designed to open intellectual and cultural windows. They might show videos to large groups and discuss them in small groups – topics like Kenneth Clarke's *Civilisation*, Bronowski's *Ascent of Man*, Hughes' *Shock of the New*. That this does not lower A Level performances is shown by the most recent results, when the pass rate was 94 per cent. In Mathematics, 74 per cent got Grade A or B. In Modern Languages, Geology and Classics all candidates passed. And this was a year when about twenty of the brighter boys had been held back by the slowing down of the Scholars' stream.

Another new building that has enriched life is the Sewell Centre, opened in 1979. It has a workshop, rooms for painting, pottery and sculpture, an art library, a printing press. In the Design classroom thirty-seven boys are preparing for Design and Technology O Level and sixteen for A Level. The centre is open seven days a week and boys can use any part in their free time, including a TIG (Tungsten Inert Gas) set-up where they can weld aluminium, stainless steel, copper, etc. Up to fifty boys are often found in here in free time, including weekends. That is one of the great advantages of a boarding school.

It is in the Sewell Centre that the Artist in Residence has his studio, a big stimulation to boy artists. His very strong and individual paintings are exhibited in the new theatre, built within Sewell's gymnasium, the corrugated erection originally intended as a place of worship for Australians.

The demand for new buildings is unsatiated. Additions in the last ten years have been legion. The Friends of Radley Trust, founded ten years ago, raised much of the money and to this was added the proceeds of a sale of land over towards Abingdon. A new Appeal has been launched to add £750,000 to the Council's £500,000. This £1,250,000 will be used to build an indoor sports complex, which will serve the local community, as well as to renovate the music school and add a small concert hall. It is also hoped to extend the number and value of Scholarships.

OPPOSITE Cheltenham College. The Library (*photo John Keeling*)

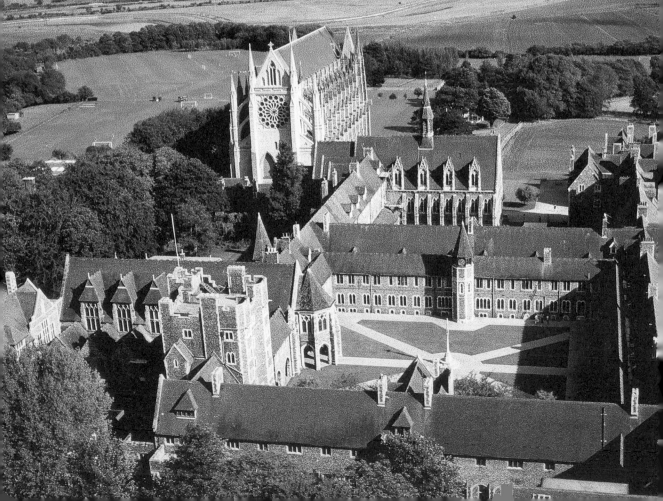

Old Radleians receive a round-robin every year from the Warden with news of the school. Nine out of sixteen members of the Council are ORs, and the fathers of 16 per cent of the boys were educated here. They can recognize a bargain when they see one; fifteen years ago Radley was one of the most expensive Public Schools, now fifty-seven of them charge higher fees. Sewell wanted to create a nice school where boys surrounded by nice things would become nice people. To make it like a University College he called his masters Fellows and made the boys wear short undergraduate-style gowns. Today's gowned masters are called Dons and the boys still wear gowns – except on hot summer days. The character and ethos of Radley in the 1980s is strong and identifiable, and this has a lot to do with the Warden. When he came here in 1968 he found a very young and brilliant staff just waiting to be given their head. Many of them are now Headmasters elsewhere. At a time when schools were abandoning compulsory daily Chapel he held the pass. Radley still has compulsory Evensong every day. It is quite a ceremony. The school prefects, or 'Pups', proceed into Chapel carrying their symbol of office, a mortarboard. Singing is lusty and at the end the boys file out past the Dons lined up in Covered Passage. Chapel does not seem to be resented and about 140 attend the voluntary communion service every Friday.

Meals are less ceremonious, and the control of table manners has become a matter for home rather than House or school. The whole school eats on a cafeteria system in Hall, built in 1912. Seating is free for all with wives and families of Dons joining in. Around the walls are portraits of Wardens and the Coats of Arms of Prefects. Breakfast is at 7 a.m., for Radleians learn to rise and begin their day's work early.

Radley resisted the erosion of tradition that was widespread in the late 1960s. The Warden declined to admit girls, though he introduced Sixth Form entry for boys from the State sector living as far away as Northampton, Sheffield and Bradford. He retained many traditions and kept discipline tight. Pups no longer beat offenders but they may impose sanctions such as going for a run, picking stones off the new golf course or a change check, which means changing frequently into different sorts of dress and reporting to a Pup. For serious offences, such as smoking, six of the best is sometimes felt to be a better punishment for the hardened offender than rustication, especially just before A Levels. The current teenage problems, especially drug-abuse, have been avoided here, not just by tight discipline but by the theme of total commitment. Boys are not left with idle hands. The policy is one of coercion into experience. Take them to the water and make them drink, see that they use the available facilities, give them reading lists, encourage

OPPOSITE ABOVE LEFT Marlborough College (*photo Peter Tinniswood*)
OPPOSITE ABOVE RIGHT Radley College. The Mansion, which once housed the whole of the school's activities (*photo Harold Metcalf ARPS*)
OPPOSITE BELOW Lancing College (*photo J. Burke, © Lancing College*)

College Boathouse on the Thames (*Gillman & Soame, Oxford*)

them to peruse *The Times*, keep them under pressure. This does not imply a harsh regime. A Social Tutor may serve cocoa to his Social every evening, helped by his wife. And the Warden invites every boy – he knows them all by name – down to his house on his birthday for a drink.

There are, of course, opportunities to relax. There is the Gaudy, an annual celebration at the end of the Summer Term, or the Social dinner, attended by parents, when the senior boy has to make a speech and a 'loving cup' is passed round, or the Social Disco, when girl-friends come. This was the part of the TV documentary which came unstuck. The Social Disco is usually a decorous affair – too decorous for TV purposes. That night the Social Tutor was called away to help with a fire in a nearby House – a fire of dubious origin. While he was away the boys and girls were only too happy to accommodate the TV people and provide the amorous clinches desired by all. Another tradition is the Mock Election, held at the same time as a Parliamentary election. It usually takes place indoors but was moved into the open air for the TV performance.

Radley is known as a leading school in the games world. Rugby is played in the Michaelmas Term and Hockey in the Lent. Rowing starts in the Lent Term and continues during the Summer when the school divides into Dry-Bobs and Wet-Bobs. There is a pack of Beagles who hunt in the winter months. The great sporting event of the year is the Rugger fixture against Wellington, which involves twenty teams from each school.

The Radleian magazine does not hesitate to be critical, inveighing, for instance, against élite cliques in the school, but its pages give a comforting picture of life at the College, and not just games – plenty of poems, prolific drama reviews, interviews with Lord Scarman (OR) and Brough Scott (OR), a note on the Radley Oak, reports of concerts and recitals. There was a nice tale from a Chinese boy whose role in Community Service had been to help at a local primary school. He'd found another little Chinese boy there and was able to bring about contact between the kid's teachers and the non-English-speaking parents. 'When I leave Radley,' he wrote, 'the thing I shall miss most is my Thursday afternoon visits to St Mary and St John's School. . . .'

Radley College

ADDRESS Abingdon, Oxfordshire OX14 2HR

FOUNDATION 1847 by the Reverend William Sewell

GOVERNING BODY The Council (9 out of 20 are ORs)

TITLE OF HEAD AND NUMBER OF TEACHING STAFF Warden + 62 (excluding visiting teachers)

TOTAL NUMBER OF PUPILS 590

NUMBER IN SIXTH FORM 230

NUMBER OF ADVANCED LEVEL CHOICES AVAILABLE 21

NAMES OF FORMS (i) Shells (ii) Remove (iii) Vth Form (iv) and (v) VIth Forms

PRINCIPAL GAMES, BY TERMS *Michaelmas* Rugby *Lent* Hockey and Rowing *Summer* Cricket and Rowing

NAMES OF HOUSES
Socials: A, B, C, D, E, F, G, H

APPLICATION AND ENTRY Registration from birth for the school, choice of Social later. Entry 13+

SCHOLARSHIPS, ETC.
Up to 20 p.a., from £300 to full fees (maximum 15 Academic, 5 Music)
Several War Memorial Bursaries for sons of Old Radleians

TOTAL ANNUAL ALLOCATION FOR SCHOLARSHIPS, ETC. *c.* £100,000

BOOK *Looking at Radley* by M. Cherniavsky and A.E. Money

Lancing College

475 BOARDING BOYS

25 DAY BOYS

27 BOARDING GIRLS ⎱ Sixth

10 DAY GIRLS ⎰ Form

FROM A SPUR OF THE SUSSEX DOWNS THAT JUTS OUT ABOVE SHORE-ham beside the valley of the Adur a church dominates the coastline. If it seems like a symbol of faith that is exactly what it is. It was constructed in the same spirit as a mediaeval abbey; the stone was quarried locally and cut by hand and much of the construction was carried out by a Master Builder, who by coincidence was named Woodard. The roof is 150 feet high and if the tower and spire had been added as planned it would have soared to 350 feet. It rests on concrete piles bored as deep as 90 feet and the interior is on the scale of the nave of Westminster Abbey. Though it still echoes to the cadence of mediaeval plainchant, this is not a fourteenth-century cathedral. It dates from 1848, and is the Chapel of Lancing College which lies almost hidden on the plateau behind it. The most ambitious school Chapel ever projected, it symbolizes one man's faith and stands as a challenge against the materialism of the modern age. For Lancing is the flagship of a group which now numbers thirty-two schools – the Woodard Corporation.

Nathaniel Woodard was called to a double vocation, first to be a Minister of the Church and second to become the greatest founder of Public Schools. His love of music and architecture developed at Oxford, as did his passion for Catholic Anglicanism.

By 1848 aged 35 he was curate of New Shoreham, seven miles west of Brighton. In those days, when the State did not provide free schooling and the wealthy sent their sons to one of the Great Schools or engaged a private tutor, Woodard saw a need to provide boarding schools for the new commercial class created by the Industrial Revolution, which would be imbued with the spirit of Anglican Christianity, and would be on the pattern of Arnold's Rugby rather than Dickens' Dotheboys Hall. He made a start in Shoreham itself. His success and his gift for raising funds soon enabled him to build a fine school at Hurstpierpoint. When he was able to acquire the site at Lancing he came back there to found the College and build the Chapel which would be the Minster of the whole network of schools he dreamed of. In 1870 he established Ardingly College specifically for poorer parents; the fee was 15 guineas a year. In 1873 he moved north to found Denstone on a donated site. Lord Brownlow offered him the site at Ellesmere in 1879 and in 1890 the Duke of Newcastle gave him the lands at Worksop. He died in 1891 but the Woodard Corporation lived on and continued to acquire new schools. In 1911 representatives of thirteen schools met at Lancing for a dedication ceremony whose splendour was worthy of the Middle Ages. In 1982, 2,200 pupils and staff of the Woodard Schools came together for a Communion Service in Westminster Abbey, and every year representatives of the thirty-two Woodard Schools meet at Lancing for a service of re-dedication.

Before he died Woodard had become a friend of Gladstone and a national figure. His schools were founded on magnificent sites and their buildings form part of the great English heritage of architecture. He believed that such surroundings could positively aid the process of education. But splendid sites and buildings generate no revenue and his schools had no other endowments. His dream of making boarding-school education available to all who desired it foundered on the rocks of hard economic reality and political hostility. Whether his other dream was fulfilled – to inspire education with Anglican Christianity – can be judged by an assessment of Lancing College today.

From below, Lancing is slightly forbidding, for you can only see the uncompleted Chapel, but when you ascend the hill you come upon this superb elevated site. Beyond the dominant Chapel the two cloistered quadrangles, on a split level, nestle into the hillside. Their grey walls provide the largest area of finished flint in England. Huge terraced expanses of green sward can now be seen below, stretching out into the College's 550 acres of meadow land. The Hall where the whole school takes meals is also on the grand scale, nearly 100 feet high, but the two quads give the enclosed atmosphere of a

Upper Quad (*photo C.J.S. Colthurst*)

Lunch in Hall (*photo Dawes & Billings, Hove*)

College. The hilltop site enables new buildings such as the Sports Centre and swimming pool to be slotted into the fall of the slope. Some way behind is the open-air theatre, a secluded spot favoured by romantic couples, and beyond stretch the Sussex Downs, offering a vast area for free-ranging boys and girls.

The original boarding Houses surround the quadrangles and the accommodation basically is as it always has been – though with all mod. cons. New boys start in houserooms where they have places very like Winchester 'toys'. At this stage they sleep in large dormitories. As they move up the school they share studies and occupy smaller dormitories and by the end of their time may have their own bed-sitters. All this varies according to the House. The best bed-sitters are in Sankey's, a House built for boys in their last term and in Manor House, a House for girls, who have been admitted to the Sixth Form for the last dozen years. The girls seem able to preserve their femininity without becoming sex symbols, and their independence without being aloof.

The atmosphere of Lancing is friendly and relaxed, the relationship between masters and boys and girls very close. Two of the features encouraging this easy relationship are the manageable size of the school and the tutorial system. After his first term each boy chooses a master, or mistress, to be his Tutor, who will keep a watching brief on all his activities throughout his school life, see him for Tutorials either in groups or individually, and write a termly report on him. Tutors are asked in these reports to comment on non-examinable activities so that pupils will get credit for a wider range of activities than their Ordinary and Advanced Level subjects.

Lancing has always been a strong Football school and its 'old boys' won the Arthur Dunn Cup in 1983 and 1984. It is the leading school in Squash Rackets, having won or been runners-up in the Londonderry Cup nineteen times from 1949 to 1980. On the aesthetic side, Art is built into the curriculum in the lower school and we find ten candidates preparing for Advanced Level in the Art Department housed in the Crypt of the Chapel. Woodard, however, was more devoted to music and indeed music is very strong here; 180 pupils learn a musical instrument, the incentive being that they have a good chance of playing in the symphony orchestra, the concert band, the junior band or the swing band. Chamber Music is an option on Wednesday afternoon. There are even Lunchtime Concerts and, of course, there is the Choir.

This takes us to the interior of the Chapel which strangely is still not completed, largely because two World Wars interfered. The Rose Window

Girl's 'pitt' (study) in the new Manor House (1981) (*photo George Laye*)

LEFT Squash (*photo C.J.S. Colthurst*)
RIGHT Sonata (*photo George Laye*)

at the West End, with its 30,000 pieces of glass, is the largest in any English church and was finished as late as 1978. The stalls of carved wood came as a gift from Eton College Chapel, another soaring edifice. This Lancing ceiling is 90 feet high and it takes a Chapel Choir of 200 voices, all male, to fill the space. The gramophone record of the Choir is the best testimonial to its excellence, and its tradition of plainsong. The Music Scholarships have attracted a high level of entrant, including the St Paul's Cathedral choirboy who recorded British Rail's 'THIS IS THE AGE OF – the train'. Sir Peter Pears is an OL, as are Nicholas Kremer, Christopher Headington, Stewart Bedford, the Music Scholar at Worcester College, and the Organ Scholar at Queen's, not to mention Tim Rice, the theatrical superstar, who opened the new theatre here in 1984. The theatre was created in the old swimming pool building, the cost having been greatly reduced because much of the tough manual work had been done by volunteer boys working under the Design and Technology master. He will be getting a new Design and Technology Centre if the Appeal Fund, now at £350,000, reaches its target of £500,000.

Godliness used to be linked to Good Learning so what about the academic record of this Woodard School? Recently the mark required at Common Entrance was raised from 50 per cent to 55 per cent. The three years allowed for Advanced Level work was reduced to two, pupils choosing three from the eighteen subjects available. The aim of the present Headmaster has been to increase the commitment of 'Lancelots' to academic study without diminishing their relaxed, friendly and socially-conscious character. In the last eight years the Advanced Level results' graph has shown a steady rise.

Year	Passes (Grades A–E)	Grades A & B
1978	83%	30%
1984	89%	44%

Nathaniel Woodard once said, 'education without religion is a pure evil'. If the founder returned today would he be satisfied that his wishes have been fulfilled?

His dream of providing low-cost boarding-school education for people of modest income faded early. In fact, research has shown that it is a limited class of people who want that kind of education, and the others don't want them to have it. Moreover, political ineptitude has thwarted the attempts of the Public Schools to forge closer ties with the Maintained sector. But what about that other dream of linking education with Anglican Christianity as symbolized by the Chapel? Today there is only one compulsory service a week, on Sunday. If this seems an abandonment of the Founder's principles one might answer that a said Eucharist takes place daily in one of the small chapels, every Monday evening a service is organized in the Crypt by pupils or staff, seventy pupils a year come for Confirmation, the Chaplain's room is at the centre of the College and is open house at any time of the day; most of all, the Sunday service is a special occasion of liturgical style. And in 1983 Bishop Trevor Huddleston here gave the first Lancing Lecture to an audience of 700. Speaking of the plight of the Third World, he said: 'There is no evidence of the *political will* in the affluent world to turn vague aspirations into reality,' and 'I do not think the Public Schools of our country are doing enough to set the record straight'.

What *is* Lancing doing?

Well, there was the Gino Watkins (OL) Malawi Expedition 1982 and 1984 (patron Bishop Huddleston). That made a link with Malosa Secondary School which subsequently joined the Woodard Corporation. Now Lancing has discovered that for £3,000 it can build, equip and staff a school in Ecuador and is raising money to do just that. It too may become a Woodard School some hundred years after Woodard's death. But nearer at home Community Service, which had shrunk to five pupils, has taken off under a new name, OUTREACH, and now involves 100 pupils aged 14 to 18. 'Outreach' has become the most popular item among the 'activities' for which Wednesday after-noons are reserved. It works both ways, taking boys and girls out into the neighbourhood and bringing local people in. Boys start in groups and then learn to handle acute problems individually. On the theme of 'some young, some old, but all happy', they go out to help the elderly, the disabled or the blind in institutions or their own homes. They give a hand at schools for the educationally sub-normal or homes for the disabled. When disabled groups come to the swimming pool they'll help them undress, get into the pool and out again. They give strawberry teas for old folk on the Lancing lawns or host a Christmas service in the Chapel. They will do quixotic things like brightening up Shorcham Station with paint and flowers. 'Clear up, cheer up.' Thus they become more socially aware and the local people come to know and to feel real affection for their young saviours. What does it matter if the occasional bad hat makes it an excuse to skive off to Brighton?

Nathaniel Woodard would rightly conclude that the school boys or girls of today are more caring than their Victorian counterparts.

A list of the Woodard Schools will be found on page 222.

Lancing College

ADDRESS Lancing, Sussex BN15 0RW

FOUNDATION 1848 by the Reverend Nathaniel Woodard

GOVERNING BODY The Provost and Fellows of the Society of SS Mary and Nicholas

TITLE OF HEAD AND NUMBER OF TEACHING STAFF Headmaster + 52 (excluding visiting teachers)

TOTAL NUMBER OF PUPILS 537

NUMBER IN SIXTH FORM 243

NUMBER OF ADVANCED LEVEL CHOICES AVAILABLE 18

NAMES OF FORMS (i) Third (ii) Fourth (iii) Fifth (iv) Sixth (v) Upper Sixth

PRINCIPAL GAMES, BY TERMS *Advent* Soccer *Lent* Soccer, Rugby, Hockey *Summer* Cricket, Athletics, Tennis

NAMES OF HOUSES
Head's, Second's, Old's, Field's, Gibbs', Sanderson's, Teme
Sankey Residence (*Sixth Form*) Manor, Handford (*girls*)

APPLICATION AND ENTRY Registration at any time, House preference may be stated. Entry 13+, or 16+ for girls

SCHOLARSHIPS, ETC.
1 Scholarship of 100% fees
1 Scholarship of 66% fees
15 Scholarships and Exhibitions of from £600 to £2,750 p.a.
3 or 4 Music Scholarships of £600 to 66% fees
6 Music Exhibitions of £350 p.a.
2 Clergy Exhibitions of £1,750 p.a.
1 Naval Exhibition of £800 p.a.

TOTAL ANNUAL ALLOCATION FOR SCHOLARSHIPS, ETC. £140,000

BOOK *Lancing College. History and Memoirs* by Basil Handford

Bradfield College

480 BOARDING BOYS

20 DAY BOYS

5 DAY GIRLS (Sixth Form)

ST ANDREW'S COLLEGE, BRADFIELD IS THE LAST OF OUR PUBLIC Schools started in the ten years from 1841 to 1850. Its Founder was the Reverend Thomas Stevens, 'squarson' of Bradfield. He may have been prompted by the desire to provide a choir for his church, which stands close to the College, but he made it clear that the school was intended for the sons of clergymen and gentlemen; the Middle Class, or rich Londoners 'in trade', were not to be admitted. He kept tight control of the school and his obsession with such restrictive ideas led to decline and ultimately bankruptcy. Restarted under Dr H.B. Gray in 1881, the school made steady progress catering now for the upper middle class. By 1914 it was large enough to lose 279 OBs killed in the four-year war. It was a somewhat rough, tough place in those pre-war years. One former pupil wrote that 'Vimy Ridge, the Somme battle and Passchendaele were a picnic compared to the Lower Fifth in 1908'.

By contrast the Bradfield of today is one of the more tolerant and friendly places and is becoming even more pleasant as accommodation is improved. Much of this was due to the headmastership of A. Chenevix-Trench (1955–63), who put sparkle and academic pep into the place. Bradfield lost him when Eton needed a new Head Master to succeed Robert Birley, and in the same way Harrow robbed them of B.M.S. Hoban. The restlessness of the late 1960s was felt acutely at Bradfield and 1969 was known as 'the year of the revolution', after which rules about compulsory runs and leave out were relaxed.

Bradfield lies astride a crossroads one mile south of the M4 on high ground between the Thames and Kennet valleys. It can be approached from four different directions. The visitor comes suddenly on the village and College in their setting of meadows, streams and woods. They fit harmoniously into a landscape which has been mercifully spared the depredations of modern development. Trees are an important feature of the scene; they mask the College from the south-west but to north-east there are views over the attractive Pang valley. The buildings are amicably disposed on the hillside, tucked away here and there, with paths (some reserved for Prefects) winding under the branches.

The Founder had architectural good manners and though his own and later buildings are not distinguished they mostly fit harmoniously into their Berkshire setting. Until 1889 the College was a single unit which had grown up around a Tudor residence known as the Manor House. Entry to the main

Aerial view taken by the Royal Navy on a demonstration visit. Paris church left foreground (*Bradfield College*)

buildings is still through an old archway which leads onward to the Terrace, with its vistas over the 185 acres of playing fields. The buildings are largely brick and flint. Dormer windows predominate, while the dark tiled roofs and inset timbers of the Tudor style give cohesion to the whole. The most interesting building is the Hall, built on the model of an English tithe barn, with a fine timbered roof and a Burne-Jones window. Meals for the whole school are now served there on a cafeteria system. The 1903 Chapel has not been universally admired. Its wide nave is unusual in a school and the rows of pews face the altar. The three-sided quadrangle behind it is architecturally pleasant, but the same cannot be said for Gray Schools, a 1930 building of grey Cotswold brick. It blocks the view from the Terrace, masking the old Parish Church and the outlook over the cricket pitches – Major, Maximus and Pit, the latter reserved for the 1st XI. During this century the campus has been extended up and down the hillside, with the addition of new board-ing Houses and teaching facilities. There are now six out-of-College Houses, of which two are recent. Additions since 1960 have included the new Music Schools, a new Maths Block and Electronics Room, as well as fives courts and all-weather tennis courts. The Art School has been imaginatively ex-tended in the old local primary school, and the Sixth Form Club uses the former village hall. The open-air, but heated, swimming pool is hidden from view close to the vast wooden gymnasium, an indoor space of about 180 by 45 feet. The biology department is now being refurbished. The current Appeal for £400,000 is to fund a new Design and Technology Centre and an all-weather games field of synthetic grass, suitable for football, hockey, tennis, volley-ball.

Classroom blocks, with the exception of Gray Schools, are not an assertive feature. Most are tucked away unobtrusively behind the flinty façades. There are no long corridors, no cloisters and consequently the place does not have an institutional feel. The Houses are quite widely dispersed. Until recently they offered rather spartan accommodation and even now some of the bedroom–studies are small and cramped. A new boy starts his time in a Houseroom with about a dozen 'horse-boxes'. After two years he shares a study with two or three others, still sleeping in a dormitory, but a smaller one. Not till he enters the Sixth Form does he enjoy the privacy of a bedroom–study. One of the priorities at Bradfield now is to improve further the accommodation in Houses, in the interests of greater privacy.

The catchment area used to extend to almost every county in England but like everywhere else it has shrunk in recent years. Most boys now live within an hour's drive – an important point since leave out on Sundays is taken by about 75 per cent. Socially the catchment is predominantly solid middle-class. Parents choose Bradfield because they do not wish their children to be subject to too much academic pressure. Paradoxically, when he was interviewed by the College magazine, Dr David Owen, an Old Bradfieldian, commented: 'At Public School you are force-fed, brought on quicker than your age, which

Armistice Day Service by the War Memorial (*photo Antony Collieu*)

The Beaumont Library (*photo Antony Collieu*)

brings on unrealistic examination results'. He also said with characteristic charm and a due sense of gratitude to those who paid his school fees: 'I would like to see private education wither on the vine'. (*Bradfield College Chronicle*, Summer 1984.) With a Common Entrance standard of 50 per cent the school cannot and does not compete to be high on the 'league table' of Oxbridge entries or Advanced Level results. Quite a number come here who have failed the more stringent requirements of, for instance, Eton. Academic pressure is not applied to pupils, who are treated very much as individuals. Every Sixth Former has an academic Tutor who is a teacher of his principal subject. Members of the Scholarship Sixth may have up to fifteen periods a week of private study – when they may work or not as they please. There is much appreciation of the General Studies course, which aims to extend education beyond the examinable subjects. The Advanced Level subject most highly regarded by Bradfield pupils is English. In 1984 there were no takers for Latin and Greek, but seven chose Religious Studies, not exactly a bread-and-butter subject. In the past many OBs have risen to high positions in the Church.

With numbers in Houses as high as seventy, Housemasters have to delegate. Some enlist the help of other masters but many prefer to delegate administrative tasks to senior boys, and of course this develops a strong sense of responsibility. On the whole, though, Bradfieldians are unassuming and friendly with little inclination to give themselves airs. At one time the large Houserooms led to rough games and bullying, but since the role of school and House prefects ('Cops' and 'Beaks') became more pastoral, this has lessened, though a sensitive boy can still feel very out of things in a House-room. Fagging nowadays consists of doing communal jobs on a predetermined basis, so that when the fagging bell goes every boy knows what he has to do. The informal relationships among boys extend to the staff, referred to as the Senior Common Room, and the word 'sir' is not heard all that frequently. There is no school uniform as such; the approved dress is grey flannels, tweed jacket, collar and tie. 'Beaks' have the privilege of wearing a coloured instead of a white shirt. All boys wear short collegiate gowns for morning schools.

Until they reach seniority boys are expected to take exercise daily. This could be a cross-country run but usually there is some sort of House league going on. Every now and then there is a Cheese – a mass run for one whole section of the school – and the annual Steeplechase is an established tradition. Association Football and Hockey are played in the winter but Cricket is really the star game here. Pit has provided more than its fair share of University and County captains and in the mid-1980s the Eleven was undefeated for two years.

1st XI on 'Pit', College Quad in background (*photo Antony Collieu*)

The five girls in the Sixth Form hardly dilute the masculinity of the school. Joint projects and dances are arranged with nearby girls' schools but the boys do not think this is enough. They regard the absence of girls as a deprivation and feel less at ease with them in the holidays than their friends at mixed schools.

If the Founder's intention was to provide a choir for his church he would be pleased that the choir today is good enough to tour several European countries, though Chapel services are compulsory only on alternate days, with a longer service on Sundays. Music is still a very important part of life here, but the school's principal claim to fame is the Greek Play.

The Bacchae (photo Gerald Pates, LBIPP, *Gloucester)*

Bradfield owes this marvellous tradition to the Head Master who came to its rescue in 1881. Dr Gray had been to Epidaurus and the Greek theatre there had planted an idea in his mind. In 1890 he acquired a chalk pit near the school. In the six months from January to July it was transformed into a replica one tenth the size of the Epidaurus theatre. The Head Master took his coat off and worked together with boys and local labourers. Since then the Greek Play has been a feature unique to Bradfield, though now it is performed only every third year, with plays by Shakespeare in the intervening years. There is keen competition to be included in the cast and auditions begin six months ahead. Applicants who have both cricket and Advanced Level commitments in the summer have to be excluded. The actors are not necessarily students of Greek – no boy was taking Greek A Level in 1984 – and recently the lead was taken by a Science specialist. The cast are provided with a three-line version of the text; on top the original Greek, in the middle a phonetic pronunciation and underneath a translation. Actors are expertly coached in the correct Erasmian pronunciation; the chorus learn to chant their lines to a musical accompaniment, preserving the compelling rhythm of the metre. Nowhere else is it possible to see a Greek tragedy in a Greek theatre in the approved language, though it is true that the o'er-spreading trees, and the ferns, ground ivy and St John's Wort give the setting an English flavour. The audience comes from far and wide. There are groups from schools, classical dons complete with text and the odd celebrity with a taste for the unusual. In all, some 7,000 people will see the play during the week it is performed. Inevitably there are a few reluctant fathers who find themselves strangely riveted by these ancient dramas whose human themes are still relevant today.

Bradfield College

ADDRESS Bradfield, Berkshire RG7 6AR

FOUNDATION 1850 by the Reverend Thomas Stevens

GOVERNING BODY The Warden and Council

TITLE OF HEAD AND NUMBER OF TEACHING STAFF Head Master + 50 (excluding visiting teachers)

TOTAL NUMBER OF PUPILS 505

NUMBER IN SIXTH FORM 200

NUMBER OF ADVANCED LEVEL CHOICES AVAILABLE 19

NAMES OF FORMS (i) The Fourth (ii) The Shell (iii) The Fifth (iv) Lower Sixth (v) Upper Sixth (vi) Scholarship Sixth

PRINCIPAL GAMES, BY TERMS *Michaelmas* Soccer *Lent* Hockey *Summer* Cricket

NAMES OF HOUSES
Lloyd, School, Army, House on the Hill, Field, Hillside, The Close

APPLICATION AND ENTRY Registration usually 2 to 3 years before entry at 13+

SCHOLARSHIPS, ETC.
1 of 80% of fees
Up to 2 of 50% of fees
Up to 5 of 20–30% of fees
Exhibitions: 4 of £450 to £600 p.a.

TOTAL ANNUAL ALLOCATION FOR SCHOLARSHIPS, ETC. £100,000

BOOK *Bradfield 1850–1975* by John Blackie

Wellington College

IN THE ARCHIVES OF THE COLLEGE IS PRESERVED THE HOOF OF A stallion. He was the last charger ridden by Wellington and a descendant of Copenhagen, the Duke's mount at the Battle of Waterloo. Wellington was born in Ireland in 1769, the same year that Napoleon was born in Corsica. By the time he died in 1852 he had become a national figure in Britain. His funeral was accompanied by all the pomp and extravagance that a ceremonious age could muster. A national monument was proposed, to perpetuate the memory of the Victor of Waterloo, the man who had saved England from the menace of Napoleon Bonaparte. What form should it take?

The Prime Minister, Lord Derby, was staying at Balmoral with Queen Victoria and Prince Albert on that 14 September when news of the Duke's death came through. Later the Queen noted in her Journal: 'Lord Derby has sketched the plan of a monument to the memory of the dear late Duke of Wellington, which is to be a College or School for the education . . . of the Orphans of Officers. The money for this, to be raised by public subscription.' Thus, from the start, Royalty was closely associated with the school, and no one more so than the Prince Consort, who had been brought up in Germany. Disraeli once described him as 'the best educated man I ever met'. His reaction to the state of education in England, as compared to the Continent, was one of amazement. It was only in the last ten years that the government had thought about providing a free secondary education for all. Arnold's resuscitation of Rugby had reconciled the serious classes to the Public Schools (though that definition was still in its infancy). Cheltenham, Marlborough, Radley, Lancing and Bradfield had all been founded in the previous decade. But the Prince was critical of their emphasis on the Classics and their neglect of the Natural Sciences, as well as of their obsession with preparing boys for Cambridge and Oxford. Wellington College was to be something different, a school that would meet the business needs of the nineteenth century and provide entrants for the military academies of Sandhurst and Woolwich.

The Charter of Incorporation passed the Great Seal in 1853. Thirty extremely distinguished Governors were appointed, headed by HRH Prince Albert, with Lord Derby as Vice-President. The funds for this Testimonial to the great soldier were raised after some hiccups. A site near Sandhurst was selected, in an isolated wilderness which had once been the haunt of highwaymen and was now a camping ground for gypsies. Until the erection of the

Criminal Lunatic Asylum at Broadmoor ten years later, the nearest building was the Royal Military College. The architect, Mr John Shaw, designed a building described variously as decorated Italian, Louis Quinze or nineteenth-century baroque. Monumental is certainly was and when it was erected – with harsh modifications – *The Times* commented that 'it lights up with its ruddy, cheerful glow the pine woods which surround it, its purple and red bricks relieved by the masonry of Bath stone.' Queen Victoria laid the Foundation Stone on 2 June 1850, 'a stirring spectacle of royal magnificence'.

Prince Albert knew that to be successful the school must provide excellence in academic education and that meant admitting sons of laymen as well as the Foundationers. The choice of a head, or Master, was all-important. The Prince sought the advice of Dr Frederick Temple, a future Head Master of Rugby and Archbishop of Canterbury. He suggested E.W. Benson, a 27-year-old Rugby master. Benson was carefully briefed by the Prince Consort and sent on a tour of German schools before taking up his appointment. The Queen officially opened the College on 29 June 1859.

Benson was starting with a clean sheet and no time-honoured traditions to trammel him, but with such a powerful President and Governors he did not have a free hand. Especially over discipline he was subject to interference and his measures against 'impurity' were criticized. He corresponded copiously with Temple and in one of his letters wrote: 'The cane is quickly over, breeds no spite, spoils no temper. *Every* other punishment I know does this.' HRH kept such a close watch that he even looked through the examination papers and remonstrated when he saw that Classics carried more marks than Maths. He also commented that the boys had to perform too many Religious Exercises. A bitter pill, this, for Benson, who had requested the building of a Chapel, which had been omitted from the original plan. But he grieved more than most when the Prince died unexpectedly in 1862, succumbing to an attack of typhoid fever. Benson prevailed for twelve more years, sleeping only between 1 a.m. and 6 a.m. He fought many battles and set the school on its road to the future. He eventually became Archbishop of Canterbury – the proper goal of Victorian Masters.

The Reverend E.C. Wickham prophesied correctly that his tenure would be described as the dull second volume of a novel. Under his successor the Reverend Bertram Pollock, 'robed in silk, majestic in appearance', Wellington knew a Golden Age, becoming a place where soldiers were educated and which Royalty graced. He gave the school a character which it has never really lost, described by a modern Master as 'a polish, a grace of manner which is difficult to define'. It fell to the fourth Master to take the school forward to World War I and the ordeal of those terrible four years. Wellington was founded to commemorate Britain's greatest soldier. Sixty-six years later, in 1918, she had to count the cost of a tradition of service to the nation. Statistics by themselves are cold but these give you pause for thought: of 3,350 Wellingtonians who served in HM's Forces, 597 were killed. Twenty-one years later another 375 freedom fighters lost their lives resisting the last

Continental tyrant. The Master was not spared. He was killed by a bomb in his own front porch in 1940. The Roll of Honour was published in 1949. Let these figures tell their own story:

BOYS WHO PASSED THROUGH THE SCHOOL IN ITS FIRST 90 YEARS 10,700
DIED FOR THEIR COUNTRY 1,300
DECORATIONS FOR GALLANTRY
   Victoria Cross 15
   Distinguished Service Order 638
   Distinguished Service Cross 34
   Military Cross 678
   Distinguished Flying Cross 46
   Distinguished Flying Medal 2
   TOTAL 1,413

(182 VCs were awarded in World War II, 5 to OWs.)

Up till 1961 Wellington was still sending more than twice as many cadets to Sandhurst as any other school, though it was never intended to be a military academy. Today it is further than ever from being a militaristic school, and the CCF is compulsory only for the first year. The Dormitories may still be named after Generals in the Battle of Waterloo and the busts of the Duke's Commanders may stare down the corridors or across the Courts. But the Master's introduction to the prospectus sets the tone of today's school. 'Sensitivity to the need to reconcile opposites is what I believe education is truly all about. It is the balancing, in due proportion, of work and play, tradition and innovation, discipline and freedom, ancient wisdom and modern knowledge, competition and the putting of others first, pride in one's own community and the readiness to involve oneself in the service of a wider community outside: "the mind – the body – the soul" . . . Notwithstanding the memory of the Great Duke and the respect due to those who have fallen in War, the daily voice of Wellington has been – and is to this day – "learn how to live".'

In a period of change in the Public Schools the College has not lagged behind. Wellington today is 'a spiritually exciting place' and the evidence of that is the tiny new Chapel – Christian but non-denominational – which is to be built underground with money subscribed by OWs and parents. (Was it by accident that the Bible on the old Chapel lectern was open at Luke v, 24?) Compulsory Chapel services are few. The lower, middle and upper school each have a separate service once a week, with an Assembly on alternate mornings. Sunday services are voluntary but all can attend four liturgical Anglican services per term. The Christian echo of this modest ration of Religious Exercises – Albert would have approved – is seen in CONTACT, the community service scheme, and the voluntary service schemes of the various Dormitories.

There are now about 60 girls doing Sixth Form studies in this school

Members of the football team, the captain on the right (*photo James McConnell*)

which was once so very masculine. Since 1978 they have had their own House in the converted sanatorium. The Master has daughters of his own and he believes that girls need a place where they can relax and be themselves. Boys are allowed into the girls' House as freely as into each other's Houses or Dormitories. The Boys' Dormitories are the original In-College 'Houses', the designer having had the foresight to partition these long chambers so that each boy had his own private bed-sitting space. They are small and provide cover from view but not from sound. The girls' accommodation is more spacious, as is that in the boys' Out-College Houses. The dining hall which feeds the In-College Dormitories has been converted to the cafeteria system.

As elsewhere the style of prefecting is positive rather than negative with the emphasis on helping rather than policing, and rules are kept to a minimum. Christian names are naturally used after the first few terms. Parents too are brought more into the affairs of the school and pupils are allowed home every three weeks.

Wellington was perhaps the first school to establish links, through its Industrial Liaison Officer, with a large number of firms. Pupils learn about industry as part of their education. In the Summer Term as many as seventy may go on attachment to firms and every term a representative team – shop-floor to board of directors – visits the school for seminars and discussions. The Art school has three large painting rooms, a pottery and sculpture department, a printing section and a computer for graphic design. It is open six days a week to meet the demand. The Library contains 17,500 books with a section for OW authors, who include Harold Nicholson and John Masters. The old classrooms – Blucher, Combermere, etc. – have been turned into games rooms as space has become available in the new Queen's Court which, though modern, does not clash with Shaw's original building for it is on a different line and is masked by trees. Opened in 1978 it embodies an open-air Greek-style theatre in a dip.

All first-year boys attend the Art school and the Design Centre, each for one and a half terms, and may then opt to do those subjects as an alternative to Latin and Geography. About fifty-five boys take Design at Ordinary Level and a few go on to Advanced Level in Design and Technology. One boy's A Level project was to design and make a device which would enable his mother to move his sister, who is a sufferer from spina bifida. In the future the Design Centre will be alongside the Science block, sharing computing and robotics, at a cost of £250,000. Wellington has little in the way of endowments and £3.5 million is to be raised by the sale of land. This will finance a big building programme, including the provision of larger bed-sitters for boys, a sample of which can be seen in the Archives room.

Pottery (*photo James McConnell*)

The Royal and Religious Foundation still has close links with Royalty, for the Visitor is Her Majesty the Queen and HRH the Duke of Kent is President. The original building with its internal quadrangles and corridors still looks out on swards, lakes, playing fields and woodlands. During a hundred and thirty years suburbia has crept closer and what was once forest and heath is now valuable building land. Wellington will yield some ground to the encroaching forces, but within a shrinking perimeter will construct new bastions to defend independence of mind, health of body and freedom for the spirit.

Wellington College

ADDRESS Crowthorne, Berkshire RG11 7PU

FOUNDATION 1853 by public subscription and Royal Charter

GOVERNING BODY The Governors (President HRH The Duke of Kent, Visitor HM The Queen)

TITLE OF HEAD AND NUMBER OF TEACHING STAFF The Master + 79 (excluding visiting teachers)

TOTAL NUMBER OF PUPILS 798

NUMBER IN SIXTH FORM 360

NUMBER OF ADVANCED LEVEL CHOICES AVAILABLE 17

NAMES OF FORMS (i) Third Block (ii) Second Block (iii) First Block (iv) Lower Sixth (v) Sixth

PRINCIPAL GAMES, BY TERMS *Michaelmas* Rugby *Lent* Hockey and Cross-Country *Summer* Cricket

NAMES OF HOUSES
Boarding Houses Benson, Stanley, Talbot
In-Houses/Dormitories Anglesey, Beresford, Blucher, Combermere, Harding, Hill, Hopetoun, Lynedoch, Murray, Orange, Picton
Waiting Houses Upcott, Douro, Heathcote, White Cairn
Girls' House Apsley

APPLICATION AND ENTRY Entry for boys at 13+, girls 16+. Foundationers elected age 9–13

SCHOLARSHIPS, ETC.
4 Foundation Scholarships, for sons of deceased officers. Fees from £60 p.a.
10 Open Awards of from £450 p.a. to 66% fees
Various closed Scholarships
Assisted Places are available

BOOK *A History of Wellington College* by David Newsome

Haileybury

464 BOARDING BOYS

70 DAY BOYS

84 BOARDING GIRLS } Sixth

12 DAY GIRLS } Form

I F YOU OMIT THE CUMBERSOME POST-CODE THE ADDRESS IS AS CONCISE as the Queen's: Haileybury, Hertford. 'Hailey' means 'a clearing in the woods'. It was on this empty Hertford Heath, twenty miles from Charing Cross, that in 1806 the Honourable East India Company built a College. It flourished for fifty years as a distinguished centre of scholarship, training generations of men destined to serve British India, many as Governors of Provinces.

It closed in 1858. A speculator bought the premises and the 500-acre estate. He sold them eventually for £18,000 to a group of local gentry who had the double aim of maintaining employment in the area and founding a Public School. The buildings they acquired survive in the Haileybury we see today. On its site 300 feet above sea level the College is surrounded by its own land as far as the eye can see; the forty acres of playing fields nearest to hand, with woods and tenanted farm land beyond. The approach via the Avenue designed by Humphrey Repton, ex-pupil of Capability Brown, is enhanced in May-time by daffodils and flowering cherry trees. It takes you through dark arch-ways into the largest academic quadrangle in Britain, a vast grassed square enclosed by low buildings of yellow-grey bricks. While they look inward, Henry Wilkes' 1806 long neo-classical façade with its Grecian columns looks outward over Terrace and field. These two features symbolize a school whose character is togetherness and whose sons have served Empire and nation in distant lands. In 1877 a Chapel was built, thrusting into the quad, its green Romanesque cupola dominating the campus. Later buildings were added outside the quadrangle. Big School, 1912, shows only its nose inside and has a colonnaded rear. An irreverent art master referred to it as Selfridges. Later study blocks, a classroom block and the 1932 Memorial Dining Hall and quad were tacked on outside the original square. Standing separately are the newer boarding Houses and such buildings as the Art School, Music School and Science Laboratories. This last was built in 1933 and refurbished in 1971; like most of these outer buildings it is of red brick. The new Geo-graphy Centre and Study Block was built as recently as 1979. An interesting Haileybury feature is the open-air swimming pool, 220 by 30 feet.

From its foundation in 1862 Haileybury prospered and with a roll of 500 it was soon regarded as one of the Great Schools. This was largely due to its links with India. The pictures in the Master's drawing-room are a reminder of this era, and even today new boys are referred to as 'New Governors'. From the start it was a Service school, rivalling Wellington and Cheltenham in the entry lists for Sandhurst. Later, its association with the RAF was especially close. Under Clement Attlee, himself an OH, there was a majority of Old Haileyburians on the Air Council. In the famous 1945 Parliament the OHs were only exceeded by the Wykehamists and Etonians. For a school comparatively new by Public School standards its tally of eminent men is extraordinarily high.

The physical aspect of the place does much to form the Haileyburian. Crucial to this is the quad; you emerge from the buildings around it and have immediate human encounters. People meet frequently and naturally in their daily patterns, apart from the four daily meetings of the whole school – three meals and one Chapel service. The old Dormitories surround the quad. This House dormitory system sometimes causes Mums to blench when they view the school. What takes them aback is that *all* the boys in these traditional Houses sleep in the same long dormitory – forty-eight of them. Each has his little 'compart', a 3-foot high enclosure round his bed space. Boys start as a junior at one end, lights out at 9.15 p.m., and finish at the other end, lights out around 11 p.m. It is very democratic and means that in a House/ Dormitory everyone knows everyone else. There is certainly a lack of privacy but boys do learn to get along with their fellows. This is a fact of life at Haileybury. It is the opposite of Eton, where even a new boy has his own room. Boys look on these things differently from adults, and an interesting judgement was given by a group of Oxbridge candidates in 1983. Offered bed-sitters in a new block, half of them elected to stay in their Dormitory. For daytime living New Governors have a desk in a DC (Dormitory class-room, i.e. the classroom of a particular Dormitory/House). They move up to a bigger space in a House Room and finally occupy a single study in a study-block elsewhere in the school. These vary from small cell-like spaces in the old blocks to pleasant rooms in the 1979 building.

These provisions do not impress the critical visitor, but Old Haileyburians are still sending their sons, and daughters. They know that it is a happy, friendly place, where there is a good balance between athleticism and culture, where the less able boy gets plenty of help academically and where some of the old values and usages are upheld. Most important is the weekday Chapel service every morning which all are expected to attend. Attitudes have changed since the 1960s. Not only are most boys here in favour of compulsory Chapel, but they actually sing with gusto, led by a choir of 150.

To change the Dormitory system would involve drastic reconstruction and Haileybury (called Haileybury and Imperial Service College since an amalgamation in 1942) is not a rich school. During the 1970s the fees were deliberately kept down and reserves fell to a low level. As late as 1972 the annual charge was only £840. Despite its prosperous-looking classical

The largest academic Quadrangle in England, built by William Wilkins in 1809, with
Herbert Baker's Dining Hall (1932) beyond (*photo J.B.W. Thomas*)

Looking across Quad from the Chapel portico (*photo Oliver Hatch*)

The Chapel and Terrace seen from the adjacent fields (*photo Oliver Hatch*)

columns the College is not well endowed, nor has it attracted large benefactions from many of its former pupils. Nearly all such money has come from Major Russell Dore, now in his 96th year, though the Haileybury Society makes grants of about £40,000 a year. The proceeds of two Appeals in 1962 and 1972 went towards providing for Haileybury's new role as a Public School aiming to meet the educational requirements of the 1980s.

The greatest change has been the admission of girls into the Sixth Form since 1973. The old sanatorium was converted to house forty-five girls in study–bedrooms for one, two or three. At the suggestion of the Archbishop of Canterbury it was renamed Alban's. At present a former boys' House outside the quad is being converted; it will be named Allenby's after a famous OH and will enable the number of girls to be increased to eighty. The emotional tensions which arose with the first arrivals has given way now to a more natural relationship. Each girl has links with one of the boys' Houses, but they have their own sports – lacrosse, hockey, netball and tennis – and are also allowed to join the CCF. They have no uniform but are expected to wear undramatic attire with a plain skirt. There are four applicants for every available place. As elsewhere they have made a special contribution to the life of the school and their academic level has been high, one of them achieving Grade A in four subjects at Advanced Level. A Haileyburian was the first girl to win a Moreshead Scholarship to the USA. (Presumably the requirement for 'marked ability in manly sports' was waived.)

The second change is intended to meet a local need for day provision in an independent school. Already some day boys are integrated in boarding Houses, going home only to sleep. A new imaginatively-styled day House, Russell Dore, has now been built to accommodate seventy pupils. Tacked on to Russell Dore is the embryo of a Lower School, entirely for day boys. It will provide for parents who want to start their sons off in a State school and transfer to an independent school at the age of 11. The entrance test is designed to assess future potential rather than present achievement. Haileybury day boys have a very full day at the school, arriving at 8.30 a.m. and leaving as late as 10 p.m. A car park is provided for the older ones. An Appeal launched in 1985 is in aid of a new Sports Centre and the enhancement of facilities for drama and design and technology.

Haileybury once had the reputation of being a tough school and indeed its

The dome of the Chapel seen above Terrace (*photo Oliver Hatch*)

LEFT Rackets court, one of the few at a public school (*photo Oliver Hatch*)
RIGHT Judo (*photo Oliver Hatch*)

Rugby XV were a hard bunch to meet; nor were Stirling Moss and Michael Bonallack easy to beat. Its sporting record is still good, and every boy is expected to take some exercise every weekday afternoon. Rowing has died out because the river has become too crowded but there has been a growth of minority sports such as archery and sailing. Haileybury won some competition in the Public Schools rackets championships every year for the nine years to 1984 and scored at least one victory in the athletics relay championships for schools. In the 1983 'Varsity cricket match the Oxford innings was opened by two ex-captains of the Haileybury XI. In recent years Art and Music have gathered strength to counterbalance the traditional athleticism. Half the school now learn a musical instrument, and a Haileybury musical evening at Sadlers Wells has become an annual event. The school which educated Alan Ayckbourn is, of course, strong on Drama, and sends a Shakespeare play on tour every year to Europe or America.

On the academic side there is no special trend, though Maths and Science are traditionally strong, Haileybury having pioneered the Combined Science O Level course. A system of Calling-Over every three weeks ensures that pupils' work is kept up to standard, while the introduction of a tutorial system for those in the Lower Sixth helps them to adjust to Sixth Form requirements. Haileybury is not oriented so strongly towards the Sixth Form as, for instance, Marlborough. The average number of passes at Ordinary Level is usually between eight and nine. Every year about 120 candidates take Advanced Level; between them these can be expected to secure about 70 passes of Grade A and about 65 of Grade B.

Of about 140 Haileyburians who left the school in a recent year, 4 left before taking O Levels, 30 left to improve their A Level performance elsewhere, 72 went on to degree or other full-time courses, 9 went into employment and 5 into the Services. Haileybury applicants for Cambridge and Oxford in 1984 won 7 Awards (5 boys and 2 girls).

Haileybury

ADDRESS Hertford SG13 7NU

FOUNDATION 1862 by local initiative, incorporated by Royal Charter

GOVERNING BODY Life Governors and Council

TITLE OF HEAD AND NUMBER OF TEACHING STAFF Master + 65 (excluding visiting teachers)

TOTAL NUMBER OF PUPILS 640

NUMBER IN SIXTH FORM 315

NUMBER OF ADVANCED LEVEL CHOICES AVAILABLE 15

NAMES OF FORMS (i) Lower School (ii) Removes (iii) Middles (iv) Fifths (v) Lower Sixth (vi) Sixth

PRINCIPAL GAMES, BY TERMS *Christmas* Rugby *Easter* Soccer *Summer* Cricket

NAMES OF HOUSES
Boys' boarding Bartle Frere, Batten, Colvin, Edmonstone, Hailey, Kipling, Trevelyan, Lawrence, Melvill, Thomason
Boys' day Russell Dore
Girls' boarding Alban's, Allenby

APPLICATION AND ENTRY Registration at any time. Entry for boys at 11+ and 13+; for girls at 15/16+

SCHOLARSHIPS, ETC.
2 of 100% of fees
2 of 50% of fees
1 index-linked for 11+ entry
Several Exhibitions/Bursaries
3 Music Scholarships and Exhibitions
1 Art Scholarship

BOOK *Haileybury 1908–1961* by R.L. Ashcroft (soon to be updated)

Clifton College

420 BOARDING BOYS
180 DAY BOYS

CLIFTON LIES TO THE EAST OF THE LIVELY CITY OF BRISTOL, WITH its bustling commercial activity, its cultural life and its University. The College is embedded in the well-favoured residential suburb of Clifton, which grew up in the nineteenth century *because* there was a Public School nearby. The Avon Gorge, spanned by the famous suspension bridge, hems it in on the west. The open fields that once surrounded the school and its now inadequate Close were bought up for house development before the rise of athleticism made playing fields so important. Next door is the Zoo, which has also expanded. Its inmates have a habit of waking up half an hour before the boys and raucously demanding food.

The College was founded in 1862, the same year as Haileybury, when a group of merchants and professional people decided that Bristol needed a school on the lines of Rugby. The buildings, of pinkish stone quarried on the spot, were put up on a collegiate plan reminiscent of Cambridge and Oxford. Many of them were given names adopted from Rugby. Victorian mock Gothic has now come back into favour, but it was a style that could dwarf the timid new boy. Seen from across the grassy sward of the Close, the Chapel, Big School and Library, School House and the arcaded Percival Building have a stylistic unity that is not broken by the 1927 Science Schools, also in a neo-Gothic style. There are none of those utilitarian accretions which litter so many school sites. The 1983 Sports Centre is tucked away so that it is almost invisible, the Coulson Maths and Technology Centre hides ultra-modernity behind the façade of an Edwardian private house, the new theatre lurks inconspicuously down a side street, Boarding Houses are indistinguishable from private residences – which many of them once were. Clifton can be grateful to its architects, less grateful to those who failed to buy up the surrounding fields before the developers moved in. The suburb has encroached on all sides except the north, where the Down and Leigh Woods still provide an outlet. A small fleet of ancient blue school buses transports the boys out to the fifty acres of playing fields at Beggar's Bush, some miles beyond the Clifton Suspension Bridge.

OPPOSITE ABOVE Wellington College (*photo James McConnell*)
OPPOSITE BELOW Bradfield College. The Greek Theatre during a performance of *The Bacchae* (*W. Hayes, Ford Ltd*)

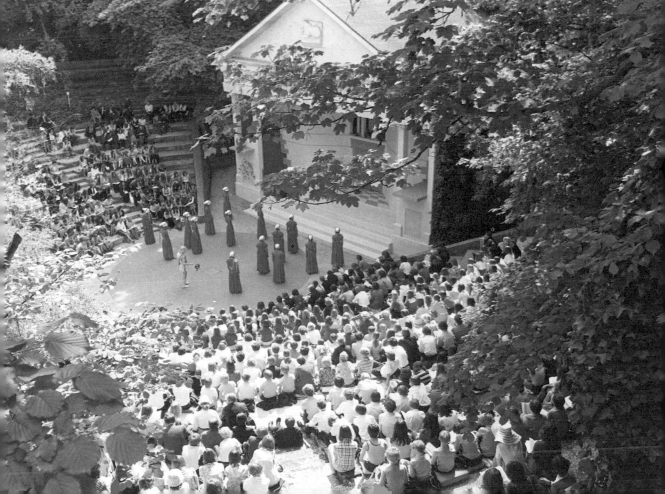

The first Headmaster had been an assistant master at Rugby. The Reverend John Percival had a formidable array of degrees – Firsts in Classics, Maths and Physics. He was no lackey of Arnold and in his own way was ahead of his time, very different from the unbending Victorian type of schoolmaster. 'It is of great importance to the life of the school,' he told his staff, 'that there should be as little as possible of a barrier between Masters and boys; that our relations with them should be not so much professional as that of friends.' That liberation, in a friendly and easy-going sense, has characterized Clifton up to the present day, and Percival's tall desk still stands in the classroom where he taught.

Percival was an anti-Tory radical, and his most important innovation was revolutionary – in the academic sense. In 1862 Science was looked down on as 'Stinks'; at Cambridge and Oxford it was not even taught by graduates. Percival put Science into the curriculum from the start, appointing two Science graduates as Masters. By 1877 Science was taught to 90 per cent of boys for up to ten periods a week, quite exceptional at the time. A distinguished line of Science teachers included Shenstone, the only man to become a Fellow of the Royal Society while still a schoolmaster, and Holmyard, of textbook fame. Of seven Professors at the Cavendish Laboratory in Cambridge, two have been OCs: Sir Nevill Mott and Sir William Pippard, the Nobel Prize winner. During the three decades from 1952 to 1981 the total number of Oxbridge Science Awards won by Cliftonians was 66, an annual average of 2.2. Clifton was a pioneer of Nuffield Science, and was ahead of other schools in offering Physics, Chemistry and Biology at Ordinary and Advanced Levels.

The original Science building was replaced by a new building opened in 1928 by the Prince of Wales. Behind its imitation Gothic stonework and fenestration it contained the most up-to-date labs and equipment of any school in the world. Today, with biology labs added on a top floor, it can still maintain that claim, by dint of shrewd buying, careful husbandry, on-the-spot maintenance and repairs. The Stone Library is unique, well-stocked with modern works and periodicals but with a collection of older books that are classics of science literature. Not surprisingly about a quarter of leavers go on to some form of Engineering or Science.

The present Headmaster is a Historian. While fostering the science tradition his key-word is balance. Thus the importance of Science is balanced by eighteen boys doing Latin and fourteen doing Greek for Advanced Level. Athleticism is balanced by all boys doing three periods of creative work per week for their first two years; thus they may discover latent talents which

OPPOSITE ABOVE Haileybury. The Avenue, leading to the main entrance (*photo Oliver Hatch*)
OPPOSITE BELOW Clifton College, The Close: *l. to r.* the original School House, Big School, the Percival Library and Wilson Tower, and the Chapel (*Clifton College*)

William Shenstone FRS (Head of Science 1880–1908) in the old Chemical Laboratory
(*Clifton College*)

The Percival Library (*Clifton College*)

they can follow up later in their spare time by doing painting, pottery, draw-ing for engineering, electronics. Hardest of all, of course, is to counter-balance the importance attached to the narrow band of subjects being studied for Advanced Level, to persuade boys to give time and attention to non-examin-able subjects. Art and Design are encouraged but it is Music that plays the most important part here. The provision of Music Scholarships and the proximity of Bristol exert their influence. The school's resources enable it to combine with a couple of other schools to stage such ambitious performances as Berlioz's *Te Deum* in a Bristol concert hall. All second-year boys do a course in the Coulson Maths and Technology Centre, but the most satisfactory results are obtained later in spare time. In the workshop boys can avail them-selves of power tools and expert guidance to do their own projects – anything from engraving to computer experiments – thus keeping alive the inventive impulse and fostering independence of thinking.

The prospectus does not over-emphasize games, though Clifton is a leading school in fencing. Rugger is played by all in the autumn, hockey and soccer are played in the spring. Cross-country running takes place in all three terms and there are ritual runs like the Winscombe and the Penpole. The summer sports are rowing and cricket. On a field near the Close in 1898 a boy called A.E.J. Collins made 628 not out in a junior House match – believed to be the highest score recorded in the history of the game. The generosity of OCs enabled the Appeal Fund to reach its target of £850,000 by 1984. Of this, £400,000 went towards the very well equipped Sports Centre with its squash courts and indoor swimming pool. Much of the rest was used to fund four new Sixth Form scholarships. Now £100,000 per year is given away in Sixth Form scholarships.

In his book *The Public Schools* (1973) Brian Gardner writes: 'Of all the Victorian Public Schools Clifton has probably produced a more varied and distinguished list of great men than any other. Its record in this respect, in little over a century, is quite remarkable.' It can be invidious to pick out 'great men' but it is interesting to follow up this statement. Colonel J.K.B. Crawford, who was at Clifton from 1921 to 1978 as boy, master and Secretary of the OC Society, recalled that when the War Memorial gateway was dedicated in 1922 those present included 2 Field-Marshals (Haig and Birdwood), 23 Major-Generals and 53 Brigadier-Generals – all OCs. More recently it is actors who have made their name: Sir Michael Redgrave (who played Lady Macbeth and Captain Surface at school), Trevor Howard, Naunton Wayne, Cecil Trouncer, John Cleese. Among musicians we find David Willcocks and Douglas Fox, among writers Joyce Carey, Geoffrey Household and John Hicks, the Nobel Prize winner. Among a legion of others there are W.O. Bentley, the car designer, Tommy Woodroffe ('The Fleet's lit up'), the poet Sir Henry Newbolt ('There's a breathless hush in the Close tonight') and Leslie Hore Belisha of Belisha Beacon fame. (He scored the winning try in Polack's first House match.)

Is there something about this school that fosters such distinction, in spite of its friendly, easy-going manner and apparent lack of *savoir faire*? Certainly there are features that make it different. There is, of course, the proximity to a great city and a top University with all the stimulus which that implies. Then there is the day-boy element; three of the ten Houses are 'Town Houses', which means that about 180 boys go back every night to their own homes, and one hopes that some of their parents' maturity rubs off on them. Two-thirds of the school in any year have come up from the Preparatory School, and are thus in a College atmosphere for double the normal period. In the fourth and last respect Clifton is unique. One House, named Polack's after its first Housemaster, is a Jewish House.

It was in 1878 that Percival decided to take the bold step of providing a boarding House for the Anglo-Jewish Community, where they could follow their own faith and have adequate instruction in it; Polack's even has its own synagogue. The Jewish community owes a great debt to Clifton and in return Polack's boys have made a big contribution, not only to the Jewish community but also to the nation. Polackians have done particularly well in music and art, but that does not mean they are laggards in sport – in one year they provided five members of the Rugby XV. Jews look for a high standard and their presence makes for keen competition, which is mostly friendly, except perhaps among the lowest age-groups.

This provision for the Jewish faith led to the flippant suggestion by a Middle Eastern OC that there should also be an Arab House. Actually there are at the time of writing five boys from Arab countries, for Clifton is very international, with about half the boarders coming from abroad, mostly from expatriate families. The contingent from India is less strong than it was – about half a dozen. The Houses seem to have different catchment areas, Polack's, for instance, being predominantly from London. The House identity is still very strong and a Cliftonian's first loyalty is to his House, in spite of the fact that the school has fed centrally in Big School since the wartime occupation by American forces. A new boarder starts by sharing a day-study with two others and sleeping in a small dormitory. He progresses to a two-boy study and larger dormitory, then shares a bed-sitter and finally has a study–bedroom to himself. As well as the Housemaster each House has a resident House Tutor and half a dozen other tutors, who come in from time to time. Perhaps the most unifying influence is the Chapel, built in 1866 in a slightly earlier Gothic style. In 1881 and 1909 a South and a North aisle were added and then Sir Charles Nicholson transformed the dull building into 'something magnificent' (John Betjeman) by adding a lantern after the style of Ely Cathedral. The pews face inwards and this adds to the sense of community. Today's boys mostly enjoy Chapel and are glad to assemble there on the four mornings a week they are required to do so, in addition to attending House prayers every evening.

Entry requirements are not stringent. All boys from the Clifton Preparatory School are admitted without having to pass Common Entrance, and there is no 'hurdle' for entry into the Sixth Form – no minimum number of

The swimming pool, part of the new sports complex completed in 1982 (*Clifton College*)

LEFT Statue of Douglas Haig, Earl Haig of Bemersyde, Commander-in-Chief of the British Armies in World War I and founder of the British Legion, with School House in background (*Clifton College*)
RIGHT Two boys with the Ark during a Sabbath morning service at Polack's House – the House for boys of the Jewish faith (*Clifton College*)

Ordinary Level passes. Once accepted on the Clifton ladder a boy may go on as far as he wants, provided he has the motivation. The curriculum allows for some O Levels to be taken at the beginning of the third year. At the end of the third year weaker boys may take seven instead of nine subjects and some may take CSE (Certificate of Secondary Education). Those weak in Science and Languages take History and Geography instead. The overall pass rate at Advanced Level, about 87 per cent recently, cannot match that of schools which have a 55 per cent pass rate at Common Entrance, a hurdle for the Sixth Form, and an influx of bright girls aged sixteen. Yet we find 100 per cent passes in ten subjects, including Latin and Greek. As the Headmaster says, 'The point of a college is that scholarly minds draw nourishment one from another.'

Clifton College

ADDRESS Clifton, Bristol BS8 3JH

FOUNDATION 1862 by Corporation, Royal Charter 1877

TITLE OF HEAD AND NUMBER OF TEACHING STAFF Headmaster + 70 (excluding visiting teachers)

TOTAL NUMBER OF PUPILS 650

NUMBER IN SIXTH FORM 230

NUMBER OF ADVANCED LEVEL CHOICES AVAILABLE 21

NAMES OF FORMS (i) Thirds (ii) Fourths (iii) Fifths (iv) Upper Fifth (v) Sixth

PRINCIPAL GAMES, BY TERMS *Autumn* Rugby *Spring* Soccer and Hockey *Summer* Cricket and Rowing

NAMES OF HOUSES
Boarding School House, Brown's, Dakyns', Oakeley's, Wiseman's, Watson's, Polack's (for Jewish boys)
Day North Town, South Town, East Town

APPLICATION AND ENTRY At 13+ or direct from Clifton Preparatory School

SCHOLARSHIPS, ETC.
9 or 10 Scholarships up to 75% of full fees for entry at 13
Several Exhibitions of lower value (may be increased in cases of need)
Awards for sons of OCs, and for the son of a newspaperman in adjacent county
Assisted Places are available for entry at 11
Music and Art Scholarships at 13
4 Sixth Form entrance Scholarships at 50% fees

Blundell's School

280 BOARDING BOYS

120 DAY BOYS

32 BOARDING GIRLS

20 DAY GIRLS

BLUNDELL'S IS THE ONLY SCHOOL IN THIS BOOK WHICH BEARS THE name of its Founder. It is an unpretentious country school which has not figured on lists of Great Schools, nor even on a recent list of 'first-rate schools'. It is seldom on the shopping list of parents who seek a Public School whose name will give a fashionable cachet to their child. But it is an example of what an independent school can achieve when the direction given from the top is enlightened and there is positive support from pupils, parents and former pupils.

It is situated away down in the West Country, 175 miles from London, and six miles beyond the motorway from Exeter to Bristol. To the north-west Exmoor and to the south-west Dartmoor enclose what has come to be known as the Blackmore Country. The present 50-acre site bestrides the main road in open country a couple of miles east of Tiverton. In the reign of Elizabeth I Tiverton was a prosperous West Country town only surpassed by Exeter and Plymouth. It owed its wealth to the cloth trade, and one boy of lowly birth made his fortune as a clothier, mostly from the Cornish kerseys he sent to London. His name was Peter Blundell, and by his Will of 1579, written in his own hand, he left money and land to provide, for the poor scholars of the town, the education that he had always lacked.

The new grammar school, its numbers limited to 150, opened in 1604. It was soon filled and for two hundred years it flourished, attracting fee-paying pupils from other parts as well as the town boys. The crisis came in the mid nineteenth century, when, as in many schools, conditions had become unduly harsh and hostility between town boys and boarders had become acrimonious. By 1847 all this had given the school a bad name and numbers shrank to seventeen. When the townspeople insisted on their rights under Peter Blundell's Will the matter had to be settled by the Court of Chancery. Its Judgement, forbidding the Master to accept boarders or fee-paying day boys, virtually abolished Blundell's chances of being a Great School. Gradually however the scheme was revised and the 'foreigners' began to return. The Endowed Schools Commission in 1861 led to the proposal that the school be moved out of the town. In 1882, in the face of intense hostility from the town, it transferred to the present site at Horsdon, where there was ample accommodation for boarders as well as day boys. These new premises had been

(photo Simon McBride, © Blundell's Public School, Tiverton)

paid for by the sale of the land bequeathed by the Founder in South Devon and at West Paule. Thus Blundell's became a First Grade school (with a leaving age of 18 to 19) and was even referred to by some as the Eton of the West.

During the 1970s the school suffered another period of decline and its public image was tarnished. Numbers fell and it became ridiculously easy to pass Common Entrance. There were even remedial classes for those whose knowledge of English was inadequate. But the approach of the centenary of the move to the Horsdon site stimulated a surge of new building and in 1980 a new Head Master was appointed. Extensions were made to all the boarding Houses and the new buildings included an Art School, Workshops, a Dining Hall for central feeding, New Big School and accommodation for Science, History, Languages and Economic Studies. A Lady Chapel was added for small congregations and private use – one of its windows marks the arrival of girls – a new Library was installed in the old Big School, renamed the Peter Blundell Room, and the allocation for new books went up from £300 a year to £3,000. Much of this was due to the fund-raising activities of the Peter Blundell Society. OBs are not noticeably rich but the appeal for £300,000 launched in 1982 had within two years passed its target. The money will go towards new Physics and Biology departments and one of the largest Sports Halls in the country.

Blundell's today is a school of 452 pupils. There are 52 Sixth Form girls of whom 32 are boarders, and about 120 day boys. With a quarter of the school coming from Tiverton, Blundell's has honoured its commitment to the local community, in contrast to a famous school which now admits hardly any day boys. The moderate size of the school means that the Head Master knows each pupil personally. He sees the whole school four times on most days: at three meals and at the daily Chapel services which all attend. In his first term each new boy brings him some object that he has made, and every boy or girl has lunch with him once every two terms. This friendliness is tempered with a warning. 'You will be issued with a copy of the School Rules. You should know and observe them. Serious offences will lead to severe punishment.'

(photo Simon McBride, © Blundell's Public School, Tiverton)

Punishments start with a reprimand, escalate to 'sides' (lines), gating (no Leaves), loss of 'own-clothes' privilege and in the worst cases rustication or expulsion. Except for the last two these sanctions are also available to School and House Monitors. In 1984 the Head of School was a girl, a unique appointment in a predominantly boys' Public School. It emphasizes the changed role of Prefect and Monitor in the 1980s.

The House and by inference the Housemaster is the principal landmark in a boy's life. The girls have their own House but are attached to boys' Houses for most activities except games. Blundell's Houses are small and manageable, only about forty to fifty in each. Each Housemaster is assisted by House Tutors and a Matron, who in many cases is his wife. An experienced master claims that he can tell which House a boy comes from merely by his behaviour and demeanour, not just by his House socks and tie. Inter-House contests generate greater rivalry and competitiveness than school matches. Housemasters, who may still use the cane as an alternative to rustication or expulsion, now go round their Houses every evening, unlike a certain previous Housemaster who had only been on the boys' side three times in fifteen years. In most Houses boys in Lower Vth (1st year) work in a Prep Room where they have a 'tosser' (desk space) and sleep in a dormitory of twelve, in Middle Vth they are in a dormitory of six and share a study, in Upper Vth they are in a double bed-sitter and in the Sixth Form have a bed-sitter to themselves. Individual accommodation may seem cramped, but there is plenty of open space – big games rooms and the former dining-rooms. In 1980 North Close was gutted by fire. Rebuilt, it is an example of what a House will be like in the future. There are links on every floor between the Housemaster's and the boys' side, the dormitories are partitioned into smaller, more private areas, and the Prep Room at the top of the House is an open, light room with views towards Exmoor. The Head of House's Sanctum is lavish; divided into bedroom and sitting-room its furniture includes a three-piece suite and a fridge. The House is carpeted throughout with fire-proof carpeting, the colour and texture of which were laid down by the Fire Officer. There are fire doors galore and a more generous provision of lavatories than before the fire.

The range of academic ability at Blundell's is wide, due to the very generous allocation for scholarships and other financial aid, a total of over £200,000 per annum. This enables many parents who could not otherwise afford the fees to enter their children. A score of day boys pay no fees at all. Not all boys are required to pass the Common Entrance Examination; Blundell's has its own entry test, usually taken by foreign children, expatriates educated overseas, or those coming from State schools. At the top end of the academic scale are the recipients of scholarships awarded on the Scholarship Examination. One Foundation Scholar, the son of a shepherd, went off the top of the scale in the Murray House I.Q. test. Competition for the available Sixth-Form girls' places and the standards required ensures that they are of above average ability.

Academic progress is regularly monitored in Common Room meetings,

(*photo Simon McBride, © Blundell's Public School, Tiverton*)

(*photo Simon McBride, © Blundell's Public School, Tiverton*)

and as much concern is shown for the diligent plodder as for the intelligent high-flyer. In the Middle School work is supervised by the Form Master, but in the Sixth Form each pupil has a work Tutor, who conducts seminars in small groups. The results at the end of the road are satisfactory considering the range of ability, about 85 per cent passing at Advanced Level. The rate for girls only is about 90 per cent, of which 40 per cent probably achieve Grades A or B. In 1984 several candidates got Grade A in four subjects. Alas, it has been found that even with Grades A1, A1, A, A, a boy may be rejected by Cambridge and Oxford. However, the school is equally proud of its humbler brethren who struggle on and leave with four passes at Grade E.

Sixty per cent go on to Higher Education with a strong trend towards Engineering – half the Sixth Form choose to do Science and Maths. Most leavers are aiming for the professions, and a significant number for the Armed Forces. In the past Blundell's has produced its famous names. We have met Archbishop Frederick Temple in earlier chapters. R.D. Blackmore, the author of *Lorna Doone*, has given his name to the whole district. Present Blundellians are proud of Jack Russell, of terrier fame. While still at school a boy called Alain John Abbott designed the statue of Christ in Blessing which fills a niche in the school tower. He died on active service with the RAF in 1943, and a replica of this statue was placed in the ruins of Coventry Cathedral by Bishop Gorton, ex-Head Master of Blundell's.

Richard Sharp, the Rugby international, exemplified the importance at Blundell's of the last great amateur sport. The great rivals are Clifton, Cheltenham, Canford and Sherborne, and enormous effort goes into the Schools Seven-a-Side at Rosslyn Park. In 1984 Blundell's were beaten in the final by Ampleforth. All boys play Rugger in the Autumn Term, while the girls play Hockey. In Spring, there is a wide choice of sports on Wednesday and Saturday afternoons. Cross-country running is well to the fore, with 'the Russell' as an annual event. In Summer, Cricket is the main game, with Tennis and Athletics also available. Tuesday is an 'activities' afternoon and Thursdays are available for community work. 'Blundell's Action' runs a number of projects to help local people, including aids for the handicapped, made in the Workshops, computer programs for the mentally handicapped, a travelling theatre and a talking newspaper for the blind. A recent Fête raised £1,600 in aid of Cystic Fibrosis.

The strong element of local day boys is evidence that Blundell's is still committed to its Founder's wishes. Some fathers have moved to Tiverton and commute long distances themselves to spare their children the daily journey. For boarders the catchment area is wide. About half come from the West Country and Bristol area, a fair number from London and a smattering from East Anglia. There are about twenty-five expatriates and an equal number of foreigners, including half a dozen Chinese, a few Germans, a couple of Africans and some American Sixth Formers. About 12 per cent of the fathers are Old Blundellians. What are these parents looking for and do they find at Blundell's what they seek?

Many are in search of what they regard as the old Public School values but within a more humane framework. They find here that rules and discipline are maintained – but by persuasion rather than harshness, the role of Monitors being to help as well as control. The old type of sentimental attraction of younger boys for older ones has naturally disappeared since the coming of the girls in 1976. A uniform dress is worn except at weekends; for boys it consists of grey flannels and either a colours blazer or a jacket of Blundell's tweed – a brown colour that blends with the brown stone buildings – while girls wear a navy-blue skirt and blazer. Sixth Form boys are allowed to wear suits on Sundays and for away matches. Beating by boys is, as elsewhere, a thing of the past and fagging only survives as a communal service or by mutual agreement on a remunerated basis. No longer do the boarders kick the day boy 'caddes' out of the school at five o'clock nor are there fights almost to the death on the Ironing-Board as described in *Lorna Doone*. But the tradition of ducking a boy in the Lowman River on his birthday is still honoured, along with the usual school slang – nobs (Monitors), sprogs (new boys) and frugals (hunger lunches for good causes).

In more abstract terms what attracts parents is the compact size of the community, its provision for locals as well as boarders, the wide range of academic ability allied to a concern that each individual should attain his or her own best level, the countrified situation far from the city's sybaritic temptations, and, not least, the insistence on daily Chapel attendance. Every

Rugby, seven-a-side (*photo Simon McBride, © Blundell's Public School, Tiverton*)

Friday this takes the form of Latin Prayers and the ceremonial is a reminder of Blundell's origin as a grammar school. All the pupils and teachers assemble in New Big School, where they stand to receive the Head Master. Then a Monitor walks up and reads in Latin the Lord's Prayer and the School Prayer. After a Latin Grace the Head Monitor calls 'School!'. The boys and girls file out, leaving the masters standing on the stage.

Blundell's School

ADDRESS Tiverton, Devonshire. EX16 4DN

FOUNDATION 1604 by the Estate of Peter Blundell

TITLE OF HEAD AND NUMBER OF TEACHING STAFF Head Master + 44 (excluding visiting teachers)

TOTAL NUMBER OF PUPILS 452

NUMBER IN SIXTH FORM 200

NUMBER OF ADVANCED LEVEL CHOICES AVAILABLE 21

NAMES OF FORMS (i) Lower Vth (ii) Middle Vth (iii) Upper Vth (iv) Lower VIth (v) Upper VIth

PRINCIPAL GAMES, BY TERMS *Autumn* Rugby *Spring* Minor games (15) *Summer* Cricket, Athletics, Tennis

NAMES OF HOUSES
Boys' boarding Francis House, North Close, Old House, Petergate, School House, Westlake
Boys' day Milestones, Thornton House
Girls' Gorton

APPLICATION AND ENTRY Boys 13+ with provision for 15/16+; girls 15/16+

SCHOLARSHIPS, ETC.
3 Scholarships of 100% fees ⎱
3 Scholarships of 50% fees ⎰ all Awards may be supplemented
3 Scholarships of 25% fees   at the Head Master's discretion
4 Foundation Scholarships, 100% tuition fees; preference to day boys resident in Tiverton
Several Music and Art Awards of up to 100% tuition fees
2 Military Bursaries of 25% fees
Other Bursaries for post-O Level, pre-Oxbridge and local residents

TOTAL ANNUAL ALLOCATION FOR SCHOLARSHIPS, ETC. £230,000+

BOOKS *The Removal of Blundell's* by J.B. Jenkins
The Making of an English Public School by M.J. Huggins

Ampleforth College

610 BOARDING BOYS

30 DAY BOYS

AMPLEFORTH IS MORE THAN A COLLEGE, IT IS ALSO A BENEDICTINE Community. The main purpose of the school attached to St Laurence's Abbey is to educate Catholics in their faith and in all branches of learning. Though it has been here only since 1802 it traces its origin to Edward the Confessor, whose Royal Abbey at Westminster was partly destroyed by Henry VIII. The Community found refuge in France till the Revolution, when the monks were again expelled. They were eventually given a home at Ampleforth by the Fairfax family of Gilling Castle. The original Ampleforth Lodge, a small house, has survived shored up by timbers into the mid-1980s. Its dilapidated appearance inspired the boys' name for their school – the Shac. Over the years it has been extended east and west along the slope of the hill and new buildings are still being added.

The flying crow finds Ampleforth eighteen miles north of the city of York on the southern fringe of the North York Moors, close to Ryedale, the Vale of Pickering and the awesome escarpment of Sutton Bank. The buildings face south looking down over The Valley, where the playing fields are laid out, with beyond them the wooded hills. A thousand acres of land stretching as far as the eye can see belongs to the Community. About two miles away is Gilling Castle, now the Preparatory School. The dominating feature of the College is the Abbey Church, completed in 1961 to Sir Giles Gilbert Scott's design.

The living and teaching accommodation has grown up higgledy-piggledy, with classrooms here, a dining-room there, 'galleries' of studies up above, a library down below. The Music School, Theatre and Junior House stand apart. The Sports Hall, the Design and Technology Centre and four of the ten boarding Houses are impressive new buildings. A unifying feature of the older part is the woodwork done by Robert Thompson of nearby Kilburn. Panelling, tables and chairs show the almost imperceptible patterns left by his adze and his unobtrusive symbol, a mouse. Internally, the long Bell Corridor extends the full length of the building, symbolizing the closeness yet separateness of the Community and the College – on the one hand the youthful activity of the boys and on the other the monks going about their daily work and worship. Each half carries on its own life, sometimes apart, sometimes together. Religion is not over-stressed, in fact there is only one school service a week on Sunday, but the boys cannot fail to notice the monks

moving in and out of their church for the half-dozen daily services laid down
by the Rule of St Benedict.

The monastery consists of about a hundred monks under their Abbot, a
successor to Cardinal Basil Hume who held the office from 1963 to 1976.
About fifty-five work out in parishes and the remainder help in one way or
another with the school. Twenty of the permanent teaching staff are monks
so the school has the advantage of a corps of free schoolmasters, a big factor
in keeping down the fees, which are the lowest of any school in this book
except Christ's Hospital. They teach not only Religious Studies and the
Humanities but also Maths, Science, Economics and Politics.

Education has always been implicit in the Benedictine tradition. The first
word of the Rule, a total plan for a monastic order laid down 1400 years ago,
was 'Listen. . . .' St Benedict's monks were soon cast in the role of teacher,
though the purpose of their way of life is *Dilatato corde*, or 'enlargement of
heart'. The Head Master still goes back to the Rule as his guide in difficult
situations, for St Benedict laid down careful guidelines on the qualities
required of the head of a community. Of course, religion pervades the life of
the place, as is seen in the reflective quality of the thrice-yearly publication
The Ampleforth Journal, largely written by monks. In it one finds, for example,
the most penetrating review of the TV serial *Brideshead Revisited* or a profound commentary on the Tibetan religion (the Dalai Lama visited Ampleforth in June 1984). Every Housemaster is a monk, and his study is a part of
the boys' House, serving also as a room which they enter without knocking,
where they can sit about and read the papers, listen to music, talk about their
problems, even telephone home. His bedroom is usually on the same 'gallery',
or passage, as theirs. Instead of a daily school Assembly, every day begins
and ends with House prayers. House common-rooms have a sliding partition
at one end. When folded back it reveals an altar, with the Sacrament, where
the Housemaster may say Mass every evening for those who wish to attend.
Thus is shown that the Sacred is never far away from the so-called Profane,
and boys are constantly in touch with a man dedicated to the highest spiritual
ideals. But this does not prevent him from being very human, ready to strip
off his habit in favour of a track-suit, or leave them to look after themselves
while he takes an audit ale with the Head Master. On the academic side the
religious dimension is emphasized by the fact that more than sixty Sixth
Formers choose Religious Studies as an Advanced Level subject.

These features apart, Ampleforth has a life very much the same as any
Public School. There is no uniform, but grey flannels and a jacket of
unobtrusive style are worn. Sport has an important place, and here Rugby
Football is paramount; the master in charge of games, John Willcox, was
Captain of England when he was appointed, and Ampleforth were victorious
in the Rosslyn Park seven-a-side festival in 1982, 1983 and 1984. They tend
to win their school matches, Sedbergh being the main stumbling-block.
There is a unique relationship between these two schools of different denomi-
nations. Not only the 1st XVs play each other, a total of seven XVs take the

ABOVE Blundell's School (*photo Simon McBride, © Blundell's Public School, Tiverton*)
BELOW Ampleforth College, with the Abbey Church designed by Gilbert Scott
(*photo Fr Christian Shore OSB*)

After Chambers, from Cannon Yard.

field. At the time of writing the accrued scores for each school are exactly equal. In the Spring Term Rugby gradually gives way to Athletics and cross-country running, and this is also the season of Beagling. The Ampleforth Beagles attract a field of about forty boys and at least as many locals. On certain meets as many as 400 locals follow the hunt. The climax of the cross-country season is a run in which all boys take part, three miles for juniors, five miles for seniors. Athletics culminates in an 8-day meeting of which the final event is the House Relay – 200 metres $\times$ 32. Cricket and Tennis are the summer sports for most, with opportunities for swimming and golf. All have to join the CCF in their first year and may continue as volunteers in their third. Scouting and the Duke of Edinburgh's Awards are well supported; in 1984 the medals gained were 4 Gold, 6 Silver and 12 Bronze.

Officially, the Common Entrance pass mark is 60 per cent, but boys from Gilling Castle and the Junior House do not sit the exam, and there are other exceptions such as younger brothers of boys already in the school. The entry is thus very strong at the top and weak at the bottom, though the story of the tortoise and the hare is often repeated by the time Advanced Levels are taken. An exceptionally generous staff ratio of 9:1 keeps classes small. As in all schools the curriculum is dominated by O and A Levels, though Remove is a haven where some can defer Sixth Form choices for a further year. For A Level there are twenty-four subjects available from which boys can make their choice, most taking three. Religious Studies and History are the individual subjects which attract the most candidates, though if you lump together those doing the different Sciences they are the greatest number. The entry for languages, apart from French, is modest, being equalled by those doing Latin and Greek, these last with excellent results. The Advanced Level results for 1984 reflect the breadth of the entry at the bottom of the school. A total of 444 papers were taken, with 3.5 per cent failing, and 40 per cent obtaining a Grade A or B (83 and 90 respectively). In the General Paper 72.5 per cent got Grade A, B or C, which may be a tribute to the time given to non-examinable subjects and General Studies. In the latest Cambridge and Oxford results, 8 Amplefordians won Awards, with 11 others gaining places; 70 more were accepted by other Universities and 10 by Polytechnics, so 100 out of 120 leavers were assured of degree courses.

The small number taking A Level Music belies the musical activity of the school. There is a Symphony Orchestra, a Symphonic Wind Band, a Chamber Orchestra and several ensembles. The Schola Cantorum is the polyphonic liturgical choir of the Abbey Church and works to a very high standard. Though Design does not yet feature in the GCE results, the subject is already being taught for examination. The new Sunley Design and Tech-

OPPOSITE ABOVE Sedbergh School. Powell House and the Chapel (*photo Robin Davey*)
OPPOSITE BELOW Eton College. School Library seen from Cannon Yard. Lithograph by Liza Andrewes (*reproduced by permission of the artist*)

The Sunley Design Centre: behind it the shored-up fabric of St Oswald's can be seen
(*photo Fr Christian Shore OSB*)

nology Centre has given a great boost to the visual arts, crafts and technical
skills. It was the subject of a separate Appeal. £600,000 was needed. One
single donor gave that amount and the Centre bears his name. It is an
imaginative building of hexagonal shape on two floors, with provision for
painting, drawing, photography, printing, electronics, metalwork, ceramics
and much more. The purpose behind it is to meet the future requirements of
industy, to explore the new technologies and to unite design, technology and
the arts under one roof. This new subject, Design, involves the use of both
mental and manual skills. It is seen at Ampleforth as a valuable academic
discipline, for it entails identifying a problem, considering various methods
of solving it and deciding on a course of practical action. The Centre has
proved immensely popular and in free time is crowded with boys. The new
breed following the Design course will gradually move up through the school.

The St Alban's Sports Hall built in 1975 stands on a knoll to the east of the
main building. It is huge in scale and contains a swimming pool as well as a
gymnasium, squash courts, etc. It is also available to local groups – over-
fifties, mums and toddlers. The former swimming pool is now an underground theatre for smaller and experimental shows. This is needed as well as
the main theatre because of the surge of interest in drama – not just goggling
at TV plays but writing, planning and acting.

Frequently these are House enterprises, for Ampleforth is closely geared
to the House system. Each of the ten Houses is named after an English Saint,

Rugger in The Valley (*photo Fr Christian Shore OSB*)

The Beagles (*photo Christopher Scrope*)

ABOVE The Dalai Lama, who visited the school in 1984, with Fr Dominic Milroy OSB,
Headmaster (left), and Fr Patrick Barry OSB, Abbot (right) (*photo Richard Henderson*)
BELOW The Abbey Church during a term-time High Mass (*photo Fr Christian Shore OSB*)

and the boys eat in their own dining-room, those in the central block being
fed from a central kitchen. Living accommodation varies considerably in
style. The older Houses are characterized by their long 'galleries', and are
not so easily identified architecturally as the new Houses, which stand in
pairs, joined like Siamese twins. The senior boys' accommodation in the
latter can compare with the most luxurious schools. After sleeping in dormitories for the first three years and working in rooms where they have individual
desk-units, Sixth Formers have their own bed-sitters, and the Head
Monitor's room verges on the palatial. Old Amplefordians, who are second
only to Etonians in their fidelity to their *alma mater* with 35.8 per cent of
boys being sons of OAs, often want their sons to go to their own old House.
They may also be influenced by the fact that their old Housemaster does not
leave the Community when he relinquishes his House – *ad volutam abbatis*.
Such a man inspired these lines in *The Ampleforth Journal*:

> from the days of your glory
>   when few moved
> with greater speed or precision
> to the days when each step
>   was a slow decision
> your life had an eloquence
>   that taught us
>   in patience
> to long for the gracious laughter
>   of a lasting Kingdom.

A nucleus of pupils come from the strong Catholic tradition in Lancashire.
There are a few from Scotland and Ireland but 60 per cent live south of a line
drawn through Watford. This may explain why, here in the hardy north, you
find boys of unusual maturity and poise. They have the easy manners and
conversation which one associates with another great school, founded by a
Catholic King. Perhaps more than in most schools the contact is kept up
between home and school. To mitigate the remoteness of Ampleforth the
Head Master and a Housemaster attend sixteen meetings a year in various
areas. They take place in the house of a parent and at the end one of the
Benedictines will conduct a Mass. In June it is the parents' turn to flock to
Ampleforth for Exhibition, when the Head Master makes his annual speech,
perhaps reminding his young listeners that 'there is something about life that
corrupts and corrodes you if you go for solutions that are easy'.

The Abbey Church had been built thanks to an Appeal in the 1950s which
raised £350,000. Another in the 1970s had provided new Houses and the
Sports Hall. In 1982 a new Appeal for £2.5 million was launched. Since then
the monk in charge of the Appeal has spoken at 500 meetings in homes or
institutions. By June 1984 the target had been reached and the total was
heading for £3.5 million, of which the average amount given has been £10,000.

How in God's name has this place been able to attract such munificence?

Well, to begin with, the giving has been to a Roman Catholic and a Benedictine Monastery rather than to a school. This money will be used to replace the crumbling and shored-up St Oswald's, the original Shac, and give the Monastery and school a new heart's core. Ampleforth feels that it has a special mission to the RC community in Britain and this belief is reciprocated. In supporting the Appeal, Cardinal Basil Hume wrote: 'There is an inherent stability in the monastic life and it is my belief that monastic witness is needed in our society as never before.' Apparently quite a few people agree with him and will put their signature on a cheque to prove it.

Ampleforth College

ADDRESS York YO6 4ER

FOUNDATION 1802. English Benedictine Community of St Laurence, with lineal connection back to Westminster Abbey

GOVERNING BODY The Abbot and Community of Ampleforth Abbey (RC)

TITLE OF HEAD AND NUMBER OF TEACHING STAFF Head Master + 76 (excluding visiting teachers)

TOTAL NUMBER OF PUPILS 625, excluding Junior House

NUMBER IN SIXTH FORM 250

NUMBER OF ADVANCED LEVEL CHOICES AVAILABLE 24

NAMES OF FORMS (i) 4th (ii) 5th (iii) Remove (iv) and (v) Middle and Upper Sixth Forms

PRINCIPAL GAMES, BY TERMS *Michaelmas* Rugby *Lent* Rugby, Cross-Country and Athletics *Summer* Cricket and Tennis

NAMES OF HOUSES
St Aidan's, St Bede's, St Cuthbert's, St Dunstan's, St Edward's, St Hugh's, St John's, St Oswald's, St Thomas's, St Wilfrid's

APPLICATION AND ENTRY At 13+ (Junior House 10+)

SCHOLARSHIPS, ETC.
Up to 6 Scholarships of from 25% to 50% fees
Up to 8 Minor Scholarships
Various special Scholarships
2 Music Scholarships
A substantial number of discretionary bursaries, awarded according to need. Some are drawn from specific Trust Funds and may vary annually.

BOOK *Ampleforth and its Origins* ed. Abbot Justin McCann and Dom Columba Cary-Elwes

Sedbergh School

424 BOARDING BOYS

16 DAY BOYS

50 JUNIOR BOYS

SEDBERGH WAS FOUNDED IN 1525 BY A PROVOST OF ETON, ROGER Lupton, as the Great School of the North of England. It has remained true to its motto *Dura virum nutrix* as a school for men. The original school house has recently been converted into a fine library. At the start of the eighteenth century this building housed the leading grammar school in the North, but by 1866 numbers had drastically slumped to a mere ten boys. After an unsparing report by the Public School Commission it revived and by 1930 numbers had risen to 400, and have remained stable near that figure.

The character of Sedbergh is moulded by the grandeur of its surroundings. It is set among the mountains of what was once the West Riding of Yorkshire, on the fringe of the Lake District. These 'fells', to give them the local name, are an enduring presence in a time of unprecedented change. In the landscape all around it Sedbergh possesses an amenity finer than any sports hall. A boy looking out at the hills through a classroom window knows that he can be out climbing them that afternoon. School and village are clustered at the foot of Winder, a hill which provides the most beautiful backdrop. The nearest town is Kendal, ten miles away, the nearest city Leeds, at a distance of sixty. There is no prep school within forty miles. But via the M6 Motorway, which passes six miles to the west, Bristol can be reached in three hours and Glasgow in two and a half.

The centrepiece of the school is the cricket pitch, with perhaps the most stupendous setting of any playing field in England. To the west and the south, on their respective knolls, stand the Chapel and the main teaching block. The other buildings, including the seven boarding Houses, are scattered around, some of them nuzzling the village. When the rhododendrons round the Chapel are in flower it is hard to remember how harsh the winters here can be. This may be why Sedbergh acquired a reputation as a 'tough' school with cold baths every morning, runs up the hills before breakfast and perpetually open windows. Things are less spartan now, but no Sedberghian is trained to be a milksop. Long before Kurt Hahn brought his Outward Bound theories from Salem to Gordonstoun the boys of Sedbergh learned to value toughness of body and spirit and knew the inspiration that could be found in the solitude of the hills. This is the most healthy of schools. It shows in the young men's faces as well as in their ready smile and greeting. Sedbergh is a small and friendly community with an unusual degree of trust and mutual respect between boys, staff and the local people. The shorts that were standard wear till a few years ago have been replaced by grey flannels, but the standard blue shirt is still worn open at the neck in all seasons. The feature that most typifies the hardiness of Sedbergh is the Wilson Run, or 'Ten', a cross-country race of more than ten very demanding miles over fell, moor and road, which was started in 1881 by a master whose name it bears. The boys of those days used to think nothing of running home at the end of term – perhaps a distance of a good thirty miles. This may explain why the record of 1 hour 10 minutes and 16 seconds, set by a now legendary hero, has stood from 1899 to the present day. But in the 1930s one boy was still running thirty miles home (he won the Ten three times) and in the 1980s the winner came within a minute of the record. Last year 122 boys competed and all of them finished, for to drop out is unthinkable. At the concert in School Hall that evening the competitors go up onto the stage in their order of finishing. The chorus of the song, 'Never shall you strive in vain in the Long Run', is sung with as much conviction by the man who finished last as by the winner.

The Ten involves individual effort. A different spirit is required for Rugby, the premier game here. The greatest Rugby player of all time, W.W. Wakefield, who chose the title Lord Wakefield of Kendal, was a Sedberghian. If it is wrong to put your whole effort, mental and physical, into a team game and develop your skills with dedication, then Sedbergh's Rugger players are blatantly culpable. Though the First XV does not tour the South, Sedbergh can justify her claim to be the greatest Rugby school in Britain. In the three years to 1984 the XV did not lose a single match and in the latter year their Captain led the English Schoolboys. The fact that this boy was an Art Scholar shows that an enthusiasm for sport need not stultify the cultural and creative instinct, may even enhance it. Sedbergh's environment gives just as much stimulus to literature, art and music as to sport. Music in particular has flourished here since the late 1930s when a Head Master decided that prestige should be given to a cultural activity in order to counterbalance the obsession with Rugger. Now one third of the boys learn a musical instrument, there is a symphony orchestra, a training orchestra, a concert band, a big jazz band, brass and string ensembles – not to mention the Chapel choir. The music staff is richly talented and a generous number of music scholarships up to the value of £2,500 is available to candidates of good quality, but these are generally ignored by preparatory schools and parents. This is a shame, for Sedbergh is a lovely place to make and listen to music. Unfortunately its reputation for manly sports blinds people to its excellence in the cultural and academic fields.

The provision of scholarships in general is generous and amounts to $4\frac{1}{2}$ per cent of the total fee income. For entry between 12.6 and 14 any number of academic Scholarships and Exhibitions up to £4,000 p.a. may be awarded, depending on the merit of candidates. A Sixth Form Scholarship to the value of £2,500 is awarded every February, in addition to five Assisted Places in the Sixth Form. A new development has been the opening of Cressbrook

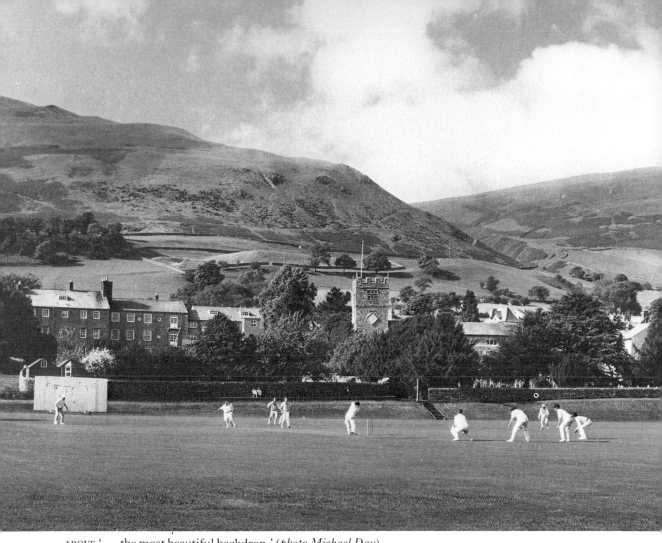

ABOVE '. . . the most beautiful backdrop.' (*photo Michael Day*)
BELOW Ten Mile Wilson Run. Left: the start 1982 (*photo courtesy The Westmorland Gazette*)
Right: On Green Hill, 1930

The main classroom block (*photo Robin Davey*)

House, a separate House with boarding provision for bright 11-year-olds from Local Education Authority schools. Four Scholarships of £2,000 p.a. plus five Assisted Places will make a Public School education available to families who would otherwise find it difficult. The scholarship examination is suited to boys who have not had the usual Preparatory School background, whose tuition fees are covered by the Assisted Places scheme, while the boarding fees are met from Sedbergh Bursaries. These Awards are now attracting good candidates from all over Britain, and boys from Cressbrook will in future form a sizeable proportion of the annual entry to the senior school.

New boys spend three or four terms working on a broad curriculum which includes all three sciences, two modern languages, and computing. Then eight subjects, one of which must be a science, are chosen for the five-term run up to O Level. As some O and A/O Levels are taken in the Sixth Form the average number of O Levels collected is ten, though entry to the Sixth Form requires five Passes. Most subjects in the lower school are streamed, so that a boy may be in the top set for one subject and the bottom set for another. A system has been introduced right through the school whereby Form Masters fulfil the role of Tutors, taking a personal interest in all aspects of their pupils' progress. Sixth Formers are given a measure of independence in the organization of their work, most of them choosing three subjects and some four. This is not a specialist school and A Level choices are spread wide. Modern Languages have always been strong here and Sedbergh has an exchange system with a French school. English and History are well supported, and new buildings in 1957, 1969 and 1974 have improved the facilities for Science. Art, Music and Design attract about half a dozen candidates each and the same number do Greek. Though Sedbergh could not vie with the schools at the top of the Oxbridge Awards league, two Awards in Classics were won in 1983. In the Sixth Form boys have three form periods a week for General Studies and their programme is diversified by two periods of Divinity, the occasional lecture on, say, History of Art and some experience of electronics and computing. Some may opt for an extra A/O Level. In the Upper Sixth they have two periods a week under their Form Master on a 'carousel' that gives them five weeks on each of five different General Studies subjects. Advanced Level results have been improving year by year and by 1984 the pass rate was 92 per cent; 8 boys achieved Grade A in three or more subjects, and of the 90 leavers 74 had three or more Advanced Level passes. 80 per cent of leavers now go on to degree courses in Universities and Polytechnics, others choosing direct entry into the Army, banking, business, catering.

The more recent buildings emphasize the advance of the less traditional subjects and the demands of a technological age. When a new complex was built in 1974 linking the sculpture, pottery and painting rooms of the Art Department with a Design and Technology Centre, Sedbergh was ahead in this very competitive field, but now that Electronics have arrived they have to be shared between the Physics and the Design and Technology Centre. The school is fortunate in possessing a particularly pleasant main teaching block, with wonderful vistas over the fells. Its carpeted corridors and classrooms, fresh paint and varnished doors, brilliant lighting and illuminated notice-boards are more suggestive of a London club than a school. Beneath the broad terrace in front of it are the Cloisters, their arches opening towards the hills. Here are inscribed the names of the 270 Sedberghians killed in 1914–18 and the 192 killed in 1939–45. A modest memorial on the terrace above commemorates three VCs of World War II, two of them won in North Africa on the same day.

Up till now funds have been spent on improving the facilities for teaching.

Now it is to be the turn of the seven boarding Houses, whose ages range from sixty to 200 years. Accommodation has in many Houses been somewhat rudimentary but now the policy is that the day-rooms of Third Formers will be made more conducive to private study, Fourth Formers will share studies of four or five, Fifth Formers of three or two, and Lower Sixth studies will be single or shared with one other. The large dormitories will be split into smaller units and all Upper Sixth boys will have individual bedroom–studies. The first conversions began in 1984 and the whole scheme should be completed by 1987.

As in all schools the catchment area has shrunk and the contingents that used to come from Scotland and Northern Ireland have dried up. Ninety-four of the boys in the school are still the sons of OSs, though some fathers may deplore the comfortable life of the modern Sedberghian compared with the tough and spartan conditions of yore. But they have to admit that the policy of a new Head Master from a more academic southern school is bearing fruit. For it has been shown that the endeavour to achieve one's highest possible performance on the Rugby field or in the Ten need not clash with the pursuit of excellence in the academic field as well, and that Sedbergh can nurture the aesthete as well as the athlete – perhaps even combining those apparent opposites in the same person.

By the River Rawthey (*photo Robin Davey*)

Sedbergh School

ADDRESS Sedbergh, Cumbria LA10 5HG

FOUNDATION 1525 by Roger Lupton, Provost of Eton

TITLE OF HEAD AND NUMBER OF TEACHING STAFF Head Master + 45
(excluding visiting teachers)

TOTAL NUMBER OF PUPILS 480

NUMBER IN SIXTH FORM 175

NUMBER OF ADVANCED LEVEL CHOICES AVAILABLE 19

NAMES OF FORMS (i) 3rd (ii) 4th (iii) 5th (iv) and (v) Sixth

PRINCIPAL GAMES, BY TERMS *Autumn* Rugby *Spring* Rugby and
Cross-country *Summer* Cricket

NAMES OF HOUSES
Evans, Hart, Lupton, Powell, Sedgwick, School, Winder
Cressbrook (Junior House)

APPLICATION AND ENTRY 11+ and 13+

SCHOLARSHIPS, ETC.
4 Junior Scholarships (age $10\frac{1}{2}$ to 12) of £2,000 p.a. plus 5 Assisted Places
15 approx.* Senior Scholarships (age $12\frac{1}{2}$ to 14), of up to £4,000 p.a., index-linked
3 approx.* Sixth Form Scholarships of up to £2,500 p.a. plus 5 Assisted Places
5 approx.* Music Scholarships of up to £2,500 p.a.
1 Art Scholarship of £1,000
* varies according to merit of candidates in any year.
Bursaries All Awards may in cases of need be supplemented up to the full
fees

TOTAL ANNUAL ALLOCATION FOR SCHOLARSHIPS, ETC. 4.5% of total fee
income

BOOK *The Wilson Run* by N.F. Berry

Eton College

1,270 BOARDING BOYS

THE COLLEGE OF OUR LADY OF ETON BY WINDSOR IS ALMOST THE largest of the Public Schools and also one of the oldest. It is probably the most famous or, in some eyes, the most notorious school in the world. In many people's minds it is associated with lords and millionaires, top hats and white ties, the Wall Game and the outrageous success of its Old Boys in the privileged walks of life. Yet the real Eton and those who work there are very different from the popular conception of the school.

Eton cannot match the glorious environment of Sedbergh, the historical associations of Canterbury, the monastic inspiration of Ampleforth or the co-educational attractions of Bedales. Charterhouse has a superior design and technology centre, Sherborne a better sports hall, Marlborough a more exciting art school and Dulwich a finer picture gallery. St Paul's and Winchester still have a slight edge academically, Christ's Hospital wear a more eccentric uniform, Wellington has won more VCs and half a dozen schools in this book charge higher fees. So why is it so successful and why does the mere mention of its name provoke such a strong reaction, whether of fervour or opprobrium? In such a short piece as this it is not possible to provide a full answer, and in any case plenty of books have been written about the place already. There is space only to sketch a quick profile, to point out some of its advantages as well as its short-comings and to correct a few wrong ideas.

This was the first great school to be founded by a King. Henry VI chose the site because his castle at Windsor looked down on Eton, standing in its meadows across the Thames, and links between school and monarchy have been close ever since. The Provost and Head Master both require Royal approval for their appointments. The Fourth of June is still celebrated as a holiday because it was the birthday of George III, who took a special interest in the day-to-day life of the College. Since the war ended in 1945 several Royals have been educated there, even though the Queen did not choose it for her three sons.

Henry VI founded it not only to provide free education for seventy boys but also as a college of priests, an almshouse and a pilgrimage church. Through the centuries all but the school and its Chapel have vanished. The number of scholars has remained constant, their fees paid in full or in part by the Foundation, for Henry VI's generous endowments are still paying dividends today, and have been augmented by substantial benefactions in the twentieth century. Gradually the number of fee-paying students has grown – to 280 in 1700, to 430 in 1800, to 930 in 1890 and to 1,200 in 1985. In a sense there are now two Etons, the seventy King's Scholars who live in the original College and the 1,200 Oppidans who live in the twenty-four boarding Houses grouped on the other side of the old Slough–Windsor road.

Since Thomas Gray, an OE, wrote his *Ode on a Distant Prospect of Eton College* the setting has changed. The sprawl of Slough and its Trading Estate hem it in on the north and the constant din of Jumbo jets emphasizes the closeness of Heathrow. The vast acreage of the playing fields is bounded after a mile and a half by the M4 motorway, while the Thames is now too polluted for bathing and often too crowded for rowing. Within the enclosed oasis of the small township that is Eton there are no long vistas as at Blundell's or Harrow. The questing eye is soon brought up short by a schoolroom block, a boarding House or the brick wall of some ancient building. It is the historic buildings which do much to create an atmosphere of heritage and tradition, for they provide fine examples of English architecture over a period of more than three hundred years from 1440 to 1766. The Chapel, a magnificent example of English Perpendicular style, was built between 1440 and 1480 and is still central to Eton life. Rarely will you find such a variety of ancient buildings – the Cloisters, School Yard, College Hall and Library, the Brewhouse, Upper and Lower School as well as the Chapel – in daily use and in excellent repair. The buildings outside College, many of them distinguished examples of modern architecture, came into being to accommodate the increasing numbers of boys sent from all over England at a time when Eton became the fashionable school for the nobility and gentry. Taken as a whole it is probably richer than any other school in its endowments, its buildings, its educational and cultural facilities. During a fifteen-year period from 1955 to 1970 about £5 million were spent on repairs to war damage, improvements to boarding Houses and new buildings. None of the cost was met from fees, it all came from the Foundation, from benefactions or from the response to an Appeal. In the 1980s the process continues, the most recent addition being twelve more laboratories, making the provision for Science as generous as in any school in the country.

Though numerically large Eton does not have the disadvantages of a big school. Each of the Houses is a separate community of about fifty boys, conscious of its own identity and ethos. They are known by the name of the House Master (Goodman's, Quibbell's, etc.) whose personality may be re-flected in the House. The boys refer to him as 'My Tutor' – in their politer moments. Because the school is so large the Head Master delegates a great deal of responsibility to House Masters. Together they can present a formid-able body of opinion, which at times has earned them the name of 'the Barons'. Each is assisted by his Dame, who is addressed by the boys as 'Ma'am'. The name survives from the days when ladies ran boarding houses in the town to accommodate Oppidans. There are no resident assistant Tutors, for in Eton Houses most of the internal administration is carried out by the Captain and Library (House Prefects). What is not generally realized is that it is the House Master, or future House Master, who accepts a boy for entry to Oppidan

Eton, always provided he passes Common Entrance. Few such men are interested in preserving the school as a place where only the wealthy can enjoy an education so richly under-written by endowments and benefactions. A manual worker is just as likely to be made welcome as a lord or a millionaire, perhaps more so, and his son's chances of being a success at Eton are just as good. It depends more on character than wealth or rank. In fact an important characteristic of Eton is its tolerance, so that there is room for all sorts to follow their own individual preferences. Every boy has his own room from the day he arrives, where he can create his personal environment, enjoy privacy and do the work set by his beaks (masters). In the evenings House Masters go round and visit boys in their rooms and this allows for a more friendly discussion of problems than an invitation to 'come to my Study after House Prayers'.

Eton is now one of the top schools academically, not just in respect of the Awards won by the Scholars, King's or Oppidan, but also the overall performance of all boys at Advanced Level. Three things contribute to this; the presence of the Scholars, the high standard of teaching and the tutorial system. The tutorial system has for long been a fundamental feature of an Eton education. Every new boy is allocated to a work Tutor, who will see him through to Ordinary Level, when he will choose a new Tutor for his Sixth Form years. Tutors take an interest in all aspects of their pupils' school life and see them for weekly sessions, which are known as 'Private Business' because beaks are free to use the time as they think most advantageous. The variety of things done is enormous, some of the more obvious being play-reading, music and art appreciation, debating and speaking, conversation in a foreign language. At the end of every term all subject reports are sent to the Tutor, who forwards them with a covering letter of his own to the House Master

Eton tries by its salary scale to attract the best teachers in the profession. Many who come make their entire career here, perhaps in due course being invited to take on a Boys' House. The teaching staff number 130, in addition to which there are forty visiting music and art teachers. All are expected to work very hard and those who cannot rise to the Eton level of dedication soon fall by the wayside. No fees are charged here for extra help with academic work and of course masters receive no pay for all their additional activities outside the classroom. Classics is no longer the dominant subject it was until 1970, though Latin is still compulsory in the lower school and a handful take Latin and Greek A Level. The single subject which attracts most candidates in the Sixth Form is English Literature, which was not taught for A Level at all in the 1960s. Perhaps it is popular because Eton devised its specification for an ideal A Level course and persuaded the Examination Board to adopt it. When you put all the Modern Languages together they form the largest

Lower School, in use since 1440

block in the UK. A smaller percentage than in most schools do Science, though this includes some of the more able scholars. The facilities are un-paralleled and the Science staff number twenty-four, plus nine full-time and four part-time technicians. It is not generally appreciated what a strong Science tradition Eton has. In 1903 Physics teachers were demonstrating the new discovery, radioactivity, and by 1914 H.G. Moseley had given the world the theory of atomic numbers. Such famous scientists as Alfred Egerton, Sir Thomas Merton, J.B.S. Haldane and T.H. Huxley were at Eton.

The Eton curriculum is similar to that at many other schools, with a broad range of subjects being taken for the first two years, narrowing down to eight elective subjects in the third. What is different is the extent to which even junior boys are expected to organize their own work and get it done on time without supervision. Rather than being made to work they learn to work by themselves, though pressure in escalating degrees of severity is brought to bear on those who fail to deliver the goods. Trials, the internal exam held at the end of term, represent a serious hurdle that must be cleared and to qualify for the Sixth Form a boy must have achieved Grade A, B or C in at least five O Level subjects. On becoming a Specialist (Sixth Former) he can make his Advanced Level choices from at least twenty-two subjects. To prevent over-specialization he must take at least one General Study from a wide and varied range of options.

Of course, the seventy King's Scholars help to pull up the academic standards of the school but the performance of Oppidans in recent years has been steadily improving, even though some have been admitted on very modest

Common Entrance marks. Last year at Advanced Level 273 candidates took a total of 805 subjects, with a pass rate of 96.4 per cent. Of these, 34 per cent got Grade A and of candidates taking the S papers 83 per cent gained 1 or 2. The pass rate in a dozen subjects, including English Literature, was 100 per cent. In seven subjects, including Mathematics, the pass rate has been 100 per cent for the last five years. The percentage of boys leaving with three or more A Levels was 89.5. Eton's bumper year for winning Awards to Cambridge and Oxford was 1980, when the score of 48 was exceeded only by Manchester Grammar School and Haberdashers' Aske's. In 1983/4, with fewer Awards available, Eton topped the list with 34. In the past three years seven such Awards have been won by girls. Eton is not co-educational but a few girls are from time to time admitted to A Level and University entrance classes.

Perhaps even more notable has been the increasing importance of music in the last twenty years. In 1964 the number of boys learning a musical instrument was 275, in 1984 it was 625, half the school. Though the abolition of the Choir School in 1968 was bitterly lamented it enabled money to be diverted to music scholarships for Oppidans, and these music scholars have made their mark. From 1972 to 1984 the number of University and Music College Awards won by Etonians was 58. Although music is a high risk career some 350 Etonians are now in the musical profession right across

Europe. The leader of the European Youth Orchestra was recently an Old Etonian.

The possibilities for extra-curricular activities at Eton are enormous. There are fifty Societies and with London only twenty miles away they have been able to attract such diverse speakers as a Greenham Common woman, Len Murray and Tariq Ali. When Solzhenitsyn spoke in College Chapel he received a standing ovation. Eton was one of the first schools to start Social Service and now about a hundred boys are involved with the problems of nearby communities. Eton Action is the fund-raising branch of Eton Social Service.

As in any school the main free-time attraction is games. The sport at which Eton has excelled is rowing, to such an extent that she can almost be described as the cradle of rowing in England. Cricket attracted much interest in the days when the Eton v Harrow Match at Lord's was a main feature of the London scene. Two forms of football, peculiar to the place, are still played. The Field Game is a mixture of Rugger and Soccer with a bully (scrum) but no handling, and is played by all in the Lent Term. The Wall Game is a mysterious and ritualistic contest confined to King's Scholars and a few Oppidans. It climaxes on St Andrew's Day in a steaming mudlark along the wall of College Field.

Not only in sport do traditions survive. When teaching, masters wear gowns over dark grey suits, with white wing collar and white bow tie. The boys still wear their distinctive dress of tail coat, striped trousers, white collar and tie, though top hats have not been part of the uniform since World War II. Idiosyncratic as this may be it is nothing to the raiment of 'Pop'. Pop is the Eton Society, a body which deals with disciplinary matters throughout the school. Some school officers are members ex-officio, the rest are elected by existing members on criteria of personality. They wear fancy waistcoats, braided tail coats, stick-up collars with white bow ties, check trousers and a floral buttonhole. They enjoy tremendous prestige among the younger boys but some elections provoke cynical comment from their peers. If bloods survive anywhere, it is here in Pop. In the past a Pop-tanning could be carried out without reference to any master, but by 1970 corporal punishment by boys had been banned, to be followed soon by the demise of fagging. But boy power is still strong and anyone coming here from another school is struck by the weight and importance of boy opinion.

Of about 250 boys leaving the school each year 70+ are gaining entry to Colleges at Cambridge or Oxford, 90+ to other Universities and about 10 to other places of further education – a total of roughly 70 per cent. The most popular destinations for those not going to University are accountancy, the land or the Forces. A survey of those who left between 1967 and 1977, based on 80 per cent (2,035) replies, showed the wide variety of occupations in which OEs are to be found. About 450 are in accountancy, stock broking, insurance or some form of banking; 206 are in the Forces, 173 on the land and 50 in the arts–entertainment world. Though forty-nine doctors replied there

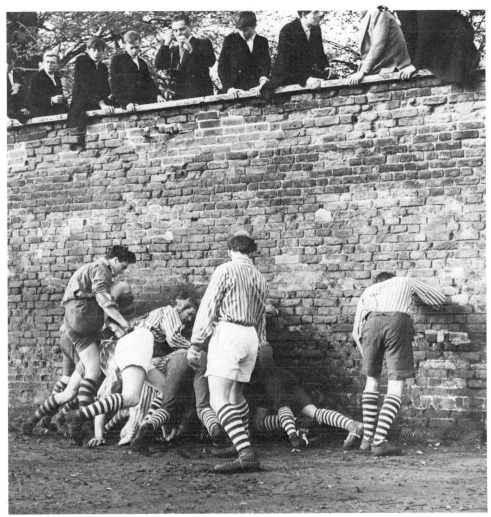

St Andrew's Day. The annual Wall Game between Collegers and Oppidans
(*photo P.S.H. Lawrence, © Sport & General (Press Agency) Ltd*)

are only seven priests, one of them the new Archbishop of York. Among a
hundred less conventional jobs the most unexpected are fireman, explorer,
commercial diver, lorry driver.

Many Etonians are drawn to political life, which is not surprising since so
much emphasis is placed on debating and public speaking. Dr Keate is famous
for flogging two hundred rebellious boys in one night, but he may also be
responsible for the rise in the standard of debate in the House of Commons
during the nineteenth century, for when he was Head Master he used to
instruct his pupils in the art of public speaking. On the Fourth of June it has
always been members of Sixth Form Select who make speeches, not the
Head Master or a visiting dignitary. That may be one reason why Eton has
provided 20 British Prime Ministers, from Walpole and Pitt the Elder to

Macmillan and Douglas-Home. OEs are always strongly represented in Parliament and the number who reach high positions in public office is disproportionate – double that of any other school. In the present century Eton can claim 5 Prime Ministers, 3 Lord Chancellors, 5 Viceroys of India, 10 Secretaries of State for Foreign Affairs, 5 Chancellors of the Exchequer. The list of famous OEs is too long to quote but includes such interesting figures as the King of Nepal, several Royal Princes, George Orwell, Lord Snowdon, Robert Bridges, Michael Bentine, Humphrey Lyttleton. Eton is specially proud to have fostered Captain Oates of the Antarctic and Colonel H. Jones of the Falklands, less proud to have produced Guy Burgess.

In World War I, 1,157 Etonians gave their lives. In World War II, when casualties were said to be so much lower, 748 were killed among the 4,958 who served in the Armed Forces, and the VC was awarded to five OEs and the MC to 355.

Is there a typical Etonian? It is not to be expected in a school where individuality has more chance to flourish than in most schools. Etonians are mentally alive and alert, eager and ready to enter into conversation or discussion. They have a natural confidence and lack of self-consciousness which makes them easy to meet. As pupils they are appreciative of good teaching even when it is applied sternly and are very loyal to their Tutors, House Masters and School. They are capable of looking at themselves and at Eton with detached judgement, as was shown when boys putting on an independent play chose *Another Country*, based on the imagined school life of Guy Burgess. The faults of Etonians are a tendency to arrogance, a sometimes maddening refusal to show enthusiasm lest it be seen as 'keenness', a somewhat materialistic attitude when it comes to choosing a career. A certain breed, rather too rich, too arrogant, too brash is often portrayed as the typical Etonian. They do exist and make their presence felt, but most OEs now keep quiet about their Old School and many never even wear the black tie with the blue stripe.

The pressure for places in the school is as great at present as it has ever been, with parents putting their sons' names down at birth. College, where the King's Scholars live, is a separate House, though they join in with the rest of the school for all activities. Entry for Scholars is by a competitive examination for boys aged 12 to 14 who need only apply a few weeks before. King's Scholars may be exempt from paying any fees. There have for long been other Bursaries for Oppidans, totalling at present up to £62,000 a year. Now, thanks to the Henry VI Educational Charity, Eton has introduced a system of Junior Scholarships, reserved for boys coming from State Primary Schools anywhere in Britain. The aim is to help parents who would not be able to meet Public School fees, and the Scholarships are awarded at age 10+ to cover two years at an independent preparatory school as well as the five years at Eton. Up to six a year are awarded and may be worth up to full fees if the parents' means justify it. At present forty Henry VI Bursaries are being provided.

The total amount of fee assistance given in one way or another by Eton College adds up to about £650,000 per annum. The extraordinary thing is that a broader and more representative section of our society has not cottoned on to the fact that Eton offers a very good bargain. But no doubt I am biased, having taught at the place for twenty-seven years.

Eton College

ADDRESS Windsor, Berkshire SL4 6DL

FOUNDATION 1440 by King Henry VI

GOVERNING BODY The Provost and Fellows (14, including 3 Honorary)

TITLE OF HEAD AND NUMBER OF TEACHING STAFF Head Master + 130 (excluding visiting teachers)

TOTAL NUMBER OF PUPILS 1,270

NUMBER IN SIXTH FORM 500

NUMBER OF ADVANCED LEVEL CHOICES AVAILABLE 23

NAMES OF FORMS (i) F (ii) E (iii) D (iv) C (v) B (vi) A

PRINCIPAL GAMES, BY TERMS *Michaelmas* Soccer and Rugby *Lent* The Field Game *Summer* Cricket, Rowing and Athletics

NAMES OF HOUSES
Houses bear the name of the House Master, e.g. D.J.S. Guilford's Esq. (or 'DJSG')

APPLICATION AND ENTRY Registration any time from birth until age 10.6, application to the Registrar or a House Master
Junior Scholars selected at 10+
King's Scholars, age 12–14, apply before Scholarship Exam each May

SCHOLARSHIPS, ETC.
15 King's Scholarships, for boys aged 12–14, of from 50% to 100% fees
6 Junior Scholarships, for boys aged 10–12 attending Local Authority schools, of 100% fees plus expenses. (Parents assessed income must be under £10,000 p.a.)
1 Anna Shaw Scholarship and 1 Oppidan Exhibition of £300–£900 p.a.
Camrose Bursaries and War Memorial Bursaries are also available and there is a remission of fee scheme for those in need.
1 Music Scholarship of 75% + of fees
3 or 4 Music Scholarships of up to 50% of fees

TOTAL ANNUAL ALLOCATION FOR SCHOLARSHIPS, ETC. £650,000 approx.

BOOK *Eton – how it works* by J.D.R. McConnell

Envoi

THE UNIVERSAL DECLARATION OF HUMAN RIGHTS ADOPTED BY THE United Nations in 1948 declared: 'Parents have a prior right to choose the kind of education that shall be given to their children'.

The TUC Labour Party Liaison Committee (Great Britain) stated: 'The changes we advocate in legislation and procedure will be introduced early in the lifetime of the next Labour Government: our aim is to abolish all private education'.

The independent schools, including the twenty-five described in this book, are again under threat. The threat is real. There are precedents for the abolition of private education; it was done by the National Socialist Party in Hitler's Germany and it has been done in the countries behind the Iron Curtain. The capital cost of a state takeover was estimated in 1980 as being about £1,500 million (Hansard 22.7.80) and the additional running costs that would be incurred by the Government at £400 million every year (ISIS figures based on 1980 statistics). In addition, the foreign currency earned by independent schools, estimated in 1981 at over £40 million, would be lost. The country would lose 129,000 boarding places, a serious deficit when the cost of placing a child in care is higher than average Public School fees.

Government policies and the imposition of the Comprehensive system led to the loss of the Grammar Schools and their Sixth Forms in the 1960s, and in the 1970s the Direct Grant Schools were swept away. It is, of course, attractive for an authoritarian type of government to gain control of *all* schools and what is taught in them. A first step against the independent schools might be the removal of charitable status and this would force them to cut the Scholarships and Bursaries which help less affluent parents. Such financial assistance enables some children to have a free education at certain schools, and is one aspect of the independent sector's long-standing campaign to make a 'Public School' education available to a wider clientele, and to strengthen links with the State system.

In spite of the stupendous cost that would have to be met by taxpayers and ratepayers, are we in Britain destined to see the nationalization of knowledge, wisdom and ethics? Will these great schools vanish as swiftly as the monasteries, abbeys and chantries did under the rapacious hand of Henry VIII? Perhaps this book gives some idea of what would be lost if the great axe were to fall.

The Author, when he was a Housemaster at Eton

Terminology

GCE The General Certificate of Education is a national examination taken by all the schools featured. Ordinary Level (O Level) is usually taken at about the age of 15 after three years in a school and Advanced Level (A Level) two years later. Candidates are graded (A, B, C, D, E or F) on their results. At A Level optional papers (S) may be taken by pupils aiming for a university. The average of passes achieved by schools in this book ranges from 87 per cent to 97 per cent.

SIXTH FORM In general terms this means pupils who have passed O Level and are doing A Level or scholarship work.

NUFFIELD SCIENCE An innovative course for Sixth Formers, worked out in collaboration between schools and the examination boards.

AWARDS Up till 1983/4 colleges at Oxford and Cambridge awarded Scholarships and Exhibitions to the best applicants for entry, but these have now been discontinued and such Awards will be made to undergraduates who do well in degree courses.

ASSISTED PLACES A Conservative Government scheme helps up to 6,000 boys and girls from any kind of school to attend an independent school.

OXBRIDGE An abbreviation of Oxford and Cambridge.

CHAPEL All the schools described have a strong element of religion, often stipulated in their foundation. 'Chapel' means not only a building but the religious services held in it.

CCF Except for Westminster and St Paul's all the schools run a Combined Cadet Force, usually with Army, Navy and Air Force sections. Boys usually join in their second or third year with an option to continue voluntarily after that. In some cases girls may join also.

PREFECTS, MONITORS, PRAEPOSTERS These are various names for senior pupils who have responsibility for administration and the behaviour and well-being of juniors.

FAGGING Until a few years ago the most junior boys in boarding schools used to perform tasks for Prefects etc., and sometimes a prefect had his personal fag who tidied his room, cleaned his shoes, made his toast and so on. Fags also played a part in the administrative machinery by carrying messages from House to House. But no longer does the stentorian cry of 'F-a-a-a-ag' or 'B-o-o-o-o-y up' ring through the corridors, and personal fagging has been replaced almost everywhere by more communal tasks.

FIVES A form of handball played in a closed court with a glove and a hard ball. Rugby Fives uses a court with straight walls, Eton Fives a court open at one end with a quirky buttress, copied from part of the outer wall of Eton College Chapel.

RACKETS Only a few schools have rackets courts, which are larger than Fives courts and have four walls. Racquets rather like extended tennis racquets are used and the game is expensive as they break so often.

BEAGLES About five schools have packs of Beagles, hounds which hunt the hare with a field that follows on foot.

LOVING CUP This is a tradition borrowed from the universities. After special dinners a silver tureen filled with wine is passed round the table, with much ceremonious bowing and scraping, even by those between whom not much love is lost.

Charterhouse (*Photo Roger Smeeton*)

Headmasters' Conference Schools

Abingdon School
Aldenham School
Alleyn's School
Allhallows School
Ampleforth College
Ardingly College
Arnold School, Blackpool
Ashville College

Bancroft's School
Bangor Grammar School
Barnard Castle School
Bedales School
Bedford School
Bedford Modern School
Belfast Royal Academy
Berkhamstead School
Birkenhead School
Bishop's Stortford College
Bloxham School
Blundell's School, Tiverton
Bolton School
Bootham School, York
Bradfield College
Bradford Grammar School
Brentwood School
Brighton College
Bristol Cathedral School
Bristol Grammar School
Bromsgrove School
Bryanston School
Bury Grammar School

Campbell College, Belfast
Canford School
Caterham School
Charterhouse
Cheadle Hulme School
Cheltenham College
Chigwell School
Christ College, Brecon
Christ's Hospital
Churcher's College
City of London School
Clifton College
Coleraine Academical
  Institution
Colfe's School

Coventry School
Cranleigh School
Culford School

Dame Allan's School,
  Newcastle-upon-Tyne
Daniel Stewart's and
  Melville College, Edinburgh
Dauntsey's School
Dean Close School,
  Cheltenham
Denstone College
Dollar Academy
Douai School, Woolhampton
Dover College
Downside School, Bath
Dulwich College
Dundee High School
Durham School

Eastbourne College
Edinburgh Academy, The
Elizabeth College, Guernsey
Ellesmere College
Eltham College
Emanuel School
Epsom College
Eton College
Exeter School

Felsted School
Fettes College
Forest School
Framlingham College

George Heriot's School,
  Edinburgh
George Watson's College,
  Edinburgh
Giggleswick School
Glasgow Academy, The
Glenalmond College
Gordonstoun School, Elgin
Gresham's School, Holt

Haberdashers' Aske's School
Haileybury
Hampton School

Harrow School
Hereford Cathedral School
Highgate School
Hulme Grammar School,
  Oldham
Hurstpierpoint College
Hutchesons' Boys Grammar
  School, Glasgow
Hymers College, Hull

Ipswich School

John Lyon School, Harrow

Kelly College
Kelvinside Academy
Kent College, Canterbury
Kimbolton School
King Edward VI School,
  Southampton
King Edward VII School,
  Lytham
King Edward's School, Bath
King Edward's School,
  Birmingham
King Edward's School, Witley
King William's College,
  Isle of Man
King's College, Taunton
King's College School,
  Wimbledon
King's School, Bruton
King's School, Canterbury
King's School, Chester
King's School, Ely
King's School, Macclesfield
King's School, Rochester
King's School, Worcester
Kingston Grammar School
Kingswood School, Bath

Lancing College
Latymer Upper School
Leeds Grammar School
Leighton Park School
The Leys School, Cambridge
Liverpool College
Llandovery College

Lord Wandsworth College
Loretto School
Loughborough Grammar
  School

Magdalen College School,
  Oxford
Malvern College
Manchester Grammar School
Marlborough College
Merchant Taylor's School
  (Crosby)
Merchant Taylor's School
Merchiston Castle School
Methodist College, Belfast
Mill Hill School
Monkton Combe School
Monmouth School
Morrison's Academy, Crieff
Mount St Mary's College

Newcastle-under-Lyme
  School
Norwich School
Nottingham High School

Oakham School
Oldham Hulme Grammar
  School
Oratory School
Oundle School

Pangbourne College
Perse School, Cambridge
Plymouth College
Pocklington School
Portora Royal School
Portsmouth Grammar School
Prior Park College

Queen Elizabeth's School,
  Blackburn
Queen Elizabeth School,
  Wakefield

Queen Elizabeth's Hospital
Queen's College, Taunton

Radley College
Ratcliffe College, Leicester
Reed's School
Reigate Grammar School
Rendcomb College
Repton School
Robert Gordon's College,
  Aberdeen
Rossall School
Royal Belfast Academical
  Institution
Royal Grammar School,
  Guildford
Royal Grammar School,
  Newcastle-upon-Tyne
Rugby School
Rydal School
Ryde School

St Albans School
St Anselm's College
St Bees School
St Benedict's School
St Columba's College
St Dunstan's College
St Edmund's College, Ware
St Edmund's School,
  Canterbury
St Edward's School, Liverpool
St Edward's School, Oxford
St George's College,
  Weybridge
St John's School,
  Leatherhead
St Lawrence College,
  Ramsgate
St Mary's College, Crosby
St Paul's School
St Peter's School, York
Sedbergh School
Sevenoaks School

Sherborne School
Shrewsbury School
Silcoates School
Solihull School
Stamford School
Stockport Grammar School
Stonyhurst College
Stowe School
Strathallan School
Sutton Valence School

Taunton School
Tettenhall College
Tonbridge School
Trent College
Trinity School, Croydon
Truro School

University College School
Uppingham School

Victoria College, Jersey

Wakefield Grammar School
Warwick School
Wellingborough School
Wellington College
Wellington School, Somerset
Wells Cathedral School
Westminster School
Whitgift School, Croydon
William Hulme's Grammar
  School
Winchester College
Wolverhampton Grammar
  School
Woodbridge School
Woodhouse Grove School
Worcester College for the
  Blind
Worksop College
Worth School
Wrekin College
Wycliffe College

The Woodard Schools

SOUTHERN DIVISION (1848)

Lancing College – boys' school with girls in VIth form; some day pupils.

Hurstpierpoint College – boys' boarding school with junior school; boarding and day pupils.

Ardingly College – boys' and girls' school and junior boys' school; boarding and day pupils.

Bloxham School – boys' school with girls in VIth form; boarding and day pupils.

St Michael's, Burton Park – girls' boarding school (11–18); some day pupils.

Tudor Hall School, Banbury – girls' boarding school.

The Archbishop Michael Ramsey School, Camberwell – boys' and girls' voluntary aided comprehensive day school (11–18) serving parts of Lambeth and Southwark.

NORTHERN DIVISION (1903)

Queen Margaret's School, Escrick Park, York – girls' boarding and day school (8–18).

Queen Ethelburga's School, Harrogate – girls' boarding school (11–18) with some day pupils.

Queen Mary's School, Helmsley, near York – girls' school (8–16); boarding and day pupils.

The King's School, Tynemouth – boys' day school (11–18) with girls in VIth form; boys junior school; kindergarten for boys and girls.

Waverley School, Huddersfield – girls' day preparatory school with senior department up to 16.

EASTERN DIVISION (1968)

Westwood House School, Peterborough – girls' school with junior school; boarding and day pupils.

Cawston College, Norfolk – boys' school (11–16); boarding and day pupils.

St James' School, Grimsby – boys' and girls' school and choir school; boarding and day with preparatory department.

WESTERN DIVISION (1897)

King's College, Taunton – boys' school with girls in VIth form; boarding and day pupils.

Pyreland Hall, Taunton – boys' preparatory school for King's College, Taunton with girls in pre-prep; boarding and day pupils.

School of St Clare, Penzance – girls' school with junior school; boarding and day pupils.

The Cathedral School, Llandaff – boys' and girls' preparatory and choir school (5–13); boarding and day pupils.

Grenville College, Bideford – boys' school; boarding and day pupils.

St Margaret's School, Exeter – girls' school with junior department; boarding and day pupils.

MIDLAND DIVISION (1873)

Denstone College – boys' and girls' school; boarding and day pupils.

Ellesmere College – boys' school; boarding and day pupils with day girls in VIth form.

Worksop College – boys' and girls' school; boarding and day pupils.

School of St Mary and St Anne, Abbots Bromley – girls' school with junior house; boarding and day pupils.

St Hilary's School, Alderly Edge, Cheshire – girls' day school with junior school and kindergarten.

Smallwood Manor, Uttoxeter – boys' Preparatory School for Denstone College; boarding and day pupils.

Ranby House School, Retford – Preparatory School for Worksop College; boys and girls; boarding day pupils.

Prestfelde, Shrewsbury – Preparatory School linked to Ellesmere College; for boarding and day boys; pre-prep department.

Derby High School for Girls – girls' day school with junior school and kindergarten.

St Michael's College, Tenbury – boys' and girls' preparatory and choir school with pre-prep department.

The Bishop of Hereford's Bluecoat School – boys' and girls' voluntary aided comprehensive day school (11–16) serving Hereford Diocese and City.

Index to text